RAPID
RESULT
REFERRALS

RAPID RESULT REFERRALS

*Powerful Tips and Ideas
to Boost Your Sales*

Roy Sheppard

A Knowledge Nugget Guide

Centre Publishing

centre

First published in 2001 by Centre Publishing
Croft House
Clapton, Midsomer Norton
Near Bath, Somerset BA3 4EB England
Tel: 00 44 (0) 1761 414676
Fax: 00 44 (0) 1761 412615
Web: www.RoySpeaks.com

A catalogue record of this book is available from the British Library

ISBN 1-901534-04-9

This book is provided as information only. Although every precaution has been
taken in its preparation, the publisher and author assume no responsibility for
errors or omissions. Neither is any liability assumed for damages resulting from
the use of the information contained herein. Neither the author or the publisher
is qualified to give advice on legal or financial matters. Readers are reminded
always to consult with appropriate professional advisers on all such matters.

Cover design by Rob Preston
Book design/layout by Antony Parselle
Original cartoons by James Bannerman
Edited by Frankie Blagden and Stuart Booth
Printed and bound in England by Biddles Ltd
Index by indexing Specialists Ltd

'Thank You' Department

So many friends, colleagues, clients and other experts in their own fields have contributed to the research, writing and editing of this book. A sincere thank you to each of you.

My specific thanks go to the following;
Kathryn and Stuart Booth who have yet again proved so invaluable at every stage of the book production process. Rob Preston at Bobcat Design for the book cover design, Antony Parselle for his ideas, care and commitment whilst typesetting this book. James Bannerman for his cartoons.

Frankie Blagden for her specific advice, insight and additional material on organisational referral systems. Peter Dykhuis for developing the PeoplePortfolio® concept on my behalf. Sue Spenceley Burch whose public relations expertise is consistently top notch.

Eric Peacock, Chairman of Hospitality Plus plc and Business Link Hertfordshire, Marion Royer at London Chamber of Commerce, Mike Burch, Business Development Director at TFL International Ltd for comments and insight following his reading of earlier drafts of the manuscript.

Jay Abraham, Philip Allen, Bob Burg, Bill Cates, Margaret Coles, David Cooper at Direct Marketing Solutions, Rick Crandall, John Cresser-Brown at Zimmer, Robert Davis, Burt Dubin, Declan Dunn, Morwenna Edwards, Shaun Freeman at Freeman & Co, Frank Furness, Emily Graham, Tim Horrox of Harmonics Communications, Julian Humphries of Robson Taylor, Wynn Jenkins, Peter Joyce of Bristol Investment Group, Scott Kramnick, Andrea Neirenberg, Marci Maheson at Llandough Hospital, Ivan Misner PhD, Chris Moon, Marie Mosely, Allan Piper of Blackstone Piper, Jim Rhode, Nigel Risner of Esteem Training, Susan RoAne, Marilyn and Tom Ross, Elly Russell at Amazon.co.uk, Mark Sheer, the late Howard Shenson, Peter Thomson.

And finally, Dawn Coombs my life-line for all those times when I am away on business, for her methodical checking and re-checking of the proofs and all those impromptu English grammar lessons she insists I need!

Contents

A Personal Message

A chronic shortage of time is almost certainly the most common challenge facing business people today. Few business owners or professional sales people can afford to waste it.

Like you, I lead a busy life. Travelling, speaking and interviewing executives at conferences, consulting and running my own business chews up my own precious time. To stay up with the latest business thinking, learning from books has always been an important part of my own personal development. However, it requires a substantial time commitment to wade through hundreds of pages to find the most useful and insightful 'Knowledge Nuggets'. Sometimes too much time; and too many authors and publishers seem to conspire against readers - by hiding this material (or leaving it out altogether)!

No wonder, research has shown that over 60% of non-fiction/business book purchases are never read from cover to cover. Readership tails off dramatically after chapter two. I wanted to write a book that a busy owner manager or sales executive could pick up and benefit from in the least time.

Rapid Result Referrals has been structured with this in mind. No matter whether your business is tiny, small, medium or large, is high, low or no-tech, this book has been edited to eliminate waffle and focus on delivering a large number of practical, easy-to-implement ideas often in a bullet point format.

All the best ideas are deliberately in the first two chapters. If you don't have the time or the inclination to read the rest of the book - that's OK with me. I'll know that you've got your money's worth if you implement any of the ideas in the first two chapters. If you choose to read on (and I hope you want to), you will benefit further from my PeoplePortfolio® Referral Plan. The most common feedback from the team of people who kindly agreed to read the book manuscript was that they sometimes felt overwhelmed by the sheer number of ideas. So, please don't be intimidated. Choose the 3-5 ideas you can work with immediately, then dip into the book again and again. Remember it's structured this way to help save you time - not to induce stress!

May I wish you many Rapid Result Referrals®.

Roy Sheppard
Bath, Somerset, England.

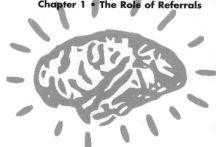

Chapter 1

The Role of Referrals

Conventional wisdom states there are only three ways to grow a business:

1) Find more customers
2) Persuade each customer to spend more each time they buy from you
3) Convince them to buy from you more often.

Rapid Result Referrals focuses on helping you find more customers or clients, regardless of your industry or the products and services you offer. With more customers, you are better equipped to maximise the potential for items two and three above.

However, many people overlook the fact that these three options not only apply to existing products and services, but to new developments. So, a fourth and potent option for growth is to move upwards or sideways into new products, services and markets. Referrals can help you to expand your 'footprint' and leap into those new areas.

Increasing sales is no longer 'desirable' for a business - it is critical. Each new customer you attract is one less for your competitors. If you don't increase the number and value of customers, your competitors will.

The full value of a new customer is far higher than most people realise. Rapp and Collins in their book *Maxi-Marketing* introduced the concept of the lifetime value of a customer.

Ask yourself these questions:-

▮ How much revenue does your average customer provide to you or your company per year?

▮ Over how many years?

▮ How much profit does each customer generate over the entire period they remain a customer?

> *Research by Lexus Cars discovered the average lifetime sales and referral value of each of their customers to be a staggering $798,454.80.*

If an average customer is worth $1,330.76 per year and remains a customer for 5 years - this customer is worth $6,653.79 to your business. Each new customer can add significant sales revenue to any business over a long period. But this represents only part of their full value. Think deeply about the next question:-

> *What could be the lifetime referral value for each of your existing and future customers?*

In some cases their referral value could be far higher than the actual revenues you earn from each customer. No matter what size organisation you work with, whether its large or small, the following example demonstrates how just one referral can lead to a long chain of other highly profitable business for you.

A long time friend is a dentist. He specialises in re-constructive surgery. A significant proportion of his considerable referral business is from other dentists. They refer patients to him for surgery outside their area of expertise.
What area of business are you or could you become a specialist in, that would generate referrals from others in your own line of business?

He once told me about just one referral chain worth tens of thousands of pounds in new business. He gives talks to other dentists on the latest technological and cosmetic procedures. One talk on restoratives and adhesives to a small group led to a referral for a half mouth re-build (value $3,326-$3,992). This referral's friend was referred and needed a bridge and crowns ($1,996-$2,661). The business partner of the referral needed a full mouth rebuild ($9,315). The wife of the first referral wanted bleaching and restorative work ($931). The wife of the business partner then wanted 20 teeth crowned and bridged ($9,315). She has three children who have all become patients. Their value as patients over the next 20 years is potentially high. This business took place in just 3-4 months and is from one referral only. It does not include any future referrals, or referrals from those referrals. Such is the awesome power of each referral chain.

And what about this question;

What is the lifetime referral value of individuals who are NOT customers?

When you add together the existing and future value of all your referrals, your business growth potential is truly exponential - but are you too busy chasing new customers to benefit from the opportunities you already have from existing ones?

Why Referrals Deserve More of Your Attention

For some, this is a new way of business. In reality, it has existed from earliest times. Additional benefits for becoming a referrals based business include:

⏵ People enjoy giving referrals - it makes them feel good about themselves to help those they like or care about.

⏵ The costs of acquiring each new customer via conventional marketing, such as advertising or direct mail, is becoming

increasingly expensive. More and more business owners and executives quietly bemoan the fact that conventional methods for finding new customers cost more than ever before, and seem to be delivering lower results. Most advertisers agree - 50% of their advertising works. The trouble is you don't know which 50%. With more competition, customer acquisition costs will go up. But not so with referrals. They are the least expensive and most profitable way to attract new clients.

⏵ Most business owners grudgingly accept that they must budget significant sums of money for advertising and direct mail, yet rarely think to allocate funds for a referral programme. Referrals can be directly tracked and measured unlike a lot of advertising. By the time you've read this book, you may choose to divert more of your marketing spend into generating referrals.

⏵ Referrals help you reduce your marketing costs in times of economic uncertainty. As competition intensifies, more and more products and services become commodities. Business owners feel forced (rightly or wrongly) to offer discounts and other inducements, to persuade prospects to do business with them. People who have been referred tend to be prepared to pay the full price for a product or service if they are confident a superior quality of service will be delivered. For example, if you're looking for a builder or a carpenter to do some work on your home, would you prefer to pay the cheapest price to someone who you don't know? Or would you pay a bit more to an individual who has been recommended by a friend or colleague whose opinions you value? Especially if she describes the worker as a person who turns up when they say they will, is hard working, uses good quality materials, the quality of the craftsmanship is high and cleans up after them. For peace of mind we will usually opt for the safer choice and pay a little more for it. Or maybe you like a 'deal' and would choose the 'cheapest' and least qualified surgeon to operate on one of your children!

⮞ Each time you receive a referral it's a confirmation that you are doing a good job in the minds of your customers - of course you do have to live up to your reputation!

⮞ Delighted customers are the best voluntary sales force you could ever have, because the power of their word-of-mouth is so immense.

⮞ Each referral gives you the opportunity to make the source of the referral (your customer) look good to their contact, therefore improving your existing relationship with that customer.

⮞ Referrals offer re-assurance to a new customer that they are not making a costly mistake. You are therefore more likely to be perceived as someone who is there to help them, rather than simply trying to profit from them.

⮞ When a high proportion of your business is derived by referral, you can be more confident that you will meet (or exceed) your sales targets.

⮞ You are less likely to suffer anxiety about where your sales will come from.

⮞ 'Time Famine' is the other scourge of modern life. We no longer seem to have the time to fully research all of our purchases. It's sometimes quicker and easier to accept the advice of trusted and knowledgeable contacts.

▶ We may feel more comfortable about achieving things on our own, but it's not nearly as effective as we need to be these days. Being more collaborative or 'interdependent' will further help to reduce your stress and improve your results.

▶ Asking for referrals in a systematic way can make a huge difference to the amount of business you are offered and therefore your commission (if you are a salesperson), or the growth of the company (if you are the owner).

> *The Freelance Survey (1998) stated that 97% of the 400 consultants and freelancers surveyed relied on contacts and referrals as one of the ways they generated business.*

▶ Micro businesses and self-employed freelancers especially, rely too much on a small number of clients. Losing key clients is potentially catastrophic for these sole traders. Being proactive about gaining referrals makes you less vulnerable - whether you are part of a small or large company.

▶ Cold calling is becoming more time consuming and less effective. In some regions around the world, legislation is even beginning to put a stop to it. If you or the company you work for, continue to rely on cold calling for the majority of your customers, your business is less likely to grow.

▶ These days, there's too much risk associated with 'buying cold'. For some, our jobs are on the line if we make poor purchasing decisions.

▶ Countless sales training courses teach you how to prospect. With limited time and its decreasing effectiveness - it doesn't make sense to prospect. The best performers don't. They devote their energy gaining quality referrals. Joe Girard was in *The Guinness Book of Records* year after year for being the world's most successful sales person. Did he cold call? No. In one year, he sold 1,435 new cars in a year - all individual sales at retail, no fleet sales and every one by referral.

▶ Leaving a voice mail message (or should that be 'voice jail'?) is more likely to be returned if someone they know has asked you to call. They won't want to risk offending that person.

▶ A claim by a third party carries far more authority and credibility than if you were to make the same claim yourself. Increasingly, cynical consumers are likely to question what you say about yourself in advertising or during presentations, yet willingly accept as fact comments from existing customers. And this is particularly true when customers are unhappy about a supplier!

▶ When people decide to contact you following a referral, you receive fewer objections. Establishing your professional authority, credibility and expertise has already been done for you by the referrer. The prospect is already thinking positively about you and your service. This has been described as shortening the 'cycle of familiarity'.

▶ Closing each sale therefore becomes easier - and quicker.

▶ With more referrals, you can start to become more selective about who you choose to do business with. Would you 'fire' your most troublesome customers? The bad ones take up an inordinate amount of your time. Your great customers end up not having the attention lavished on them that they deserve. That can't be right.

▮ With each new referral, you widen your circle of contacts. Every new person you meet has the potential to give you access to everyone within their network and are the source of dozens more referrals.

▮ Being seen to know the 'best' suppliers reflects well on us. Years ago, I was involved in producing a TV pilot show. On the day, we received a call to say that one of the key celebrity guests was unable to reach the studio in time. Panic. The show was now in jeopardy. *"I know a commercial helicopter pilot, I'll call him."* He agreed to pick up the football star and drop him at the TV studio in time for the show to go ahead. That made me look so good!

> *Successful and famous people rely on referrals. Take Martin Kemp, the former British pop star and award winning actor in BBC TVs soap, EastEnders. This story was told on the show This is Your Life. One day he mentioned to Shirley, his wife how much he would like to work on EastEnders. She used to be a backing singer in "Wham!" with George Michael. She called George, who then called his friend, the actress, Michelle Collins, who used to be in EastEnders. She called the producer and Kemp was hired. Referrals from high calibre people get things done! But you don't have to be famous to benefit from this way of doing business.*

▮ In Bill Cates's book, *Unlimited Referrals* he describes a study conducted by Chris Faicco of North Western Mutual Life in the United States. The study started with 5640 qualified suspects. 2240 were turned into prospects by cold calls. 3400 became prospects by referral. Cold call prospects made 56 sales (11%

closing ratio). Referral prospects made 452 Sales (40% closing ratio).

⫸ And most importantly of all, giving and receiving referrals is so much fun.

On the face of it, the argument in favour of using referrals is powerful. In reality, there's a great deal of resistance in adopting them as a proactive way of running a business.

As we've seen, each new referral has the power to grow your business exponentially. Think about what it would mean if every one of your customers generated three new customers. Each one of those customers could also produce three new customers, etc, etc. Carry the maths too far and there aren't enough people on the planet to become customers! However, this way of thinking has been the basis of a highly successful (and sometimes controversial) way to run a business.

The revenues and success of the Multi Level Marketing (MLM) sector cannot be overlooked. Their entire business model is based on the power of referrals and word-of-mouth.

Amway	$5 billion turnover	3 million distributors
Avon	$5 billion	3 million distributors
Tupperware	$1.05 billion	1 million distributors

There are good MLM companies and bad ones. The good ones have transformed the personal fortunes of a growing number of people dissatisfied at remaining a wage slave. A childhood friend told how Amway even saved his marriage when he turned to direct selling following redundancy.

Such is the power of word-of-mouth, some companies have tarnished the direct selling industry with irresponsible, disrespectful and even illegal behaviour. Similarly, over-zealous life insurance sales people have added to the negativity that is sometimes associated with referrals, by persuading their customers through intimidation and bullying to hand over the names of their family, friends and colleagues. No wonder referrals have earned such a bad reputation for some.

I distinctly remember meeting a casual acquaintance who had joined the finance industry in the late 1970's. I was marched into an office, sat in a chair in the middle of the room and put under increasing pressure by his bowtie wearing associate to give the names and phone numbers of everyone I knew. For years afterwards I avoided financial sales people whenever possible and refused to adopt a referrals mindset for my own business, because I 'knew' it was the 'unethical' thing to do. I was wrong. It took me a long time to realise that your best customers and clients actually want to thank you and help grow your business. They wanted to refer me to their friends and colleagues. It made them feel good and look good to the people they knew. So, let your customers and clients say *"thank you"* by recommending you to others too.

At my seminars, the owners of small and medium sized companies and the highest performing sales people state consistently that most of their business comes via referrals. Well run companies have systems for administration, recruitment, Information Technology, and just about every other business function, yet very few have a system in place for the one thing that gets them the majority of their business - referrals. Does your business plan include a section on how to generate business from your contacts and your existing customers?

It's brilliant when we receive referrals 'out of the blue'. Too many businesses treat referrals as 'unexpected bonuses'. They needn't be if you have a referral strategy. Expect them. Encourage them. You have the choice - you can benefit from referrals if and when they come your way or you can help the process by building a system.

But so many of us prefer not to ask for referrals. It often makes us feel uncomfortable. We don't want to appear too pushy, or in the case of 'professionals' or 'crafts people', we sometimes perceive it as crass, unprofessional, signalling desperation or it is in some way 'beneath us'. Professionals sometimes look down on selling and even perceive it as clashing with their professional integrity and values.

Here's the great news

Developing a business in which your customers are motivated to offer valuable referrals can only occur when you enjoy a high trust relationship. In the next chapter you will discover a multitude of ways to generate high quality referral business, without compromising your integrity. You can dramatically increase the number and quality of referrals you are offered, whilst feeling good about it, even if you 'hate' to sell. Choose the most appropriate ideas for your own specific circumstances. They work - and they can work for you.

The PeoplePortfolio® Referral Plan for Organisations

As you will now be aware, offering and asking for referrals as an integral part of your job, whether you are a sole trader, owner manager or a salesperson, will certainly improve your results. However, the real power of the PeoplePortfolio® Referral Plan occurs when a company (of whatever size) develops a collective understanding, referral mindset and implementation strategy. This is unlikely to occur unless there is a top level commitment combined with an operational framework within the company to recognise, empower and reward those who choose to participate. Increasingly, as non-sales staff develop such close working relationships with customers, they are particularly well placed to solicit referrals if motivated and trained to do so. This poses a number of profound questions for any organisation.

▶ Are staff merely paid to perform a narrow range of tasks, or are they encouraged to assume additional responsibilities, such as helping the business to grow?

◗ How do you reward such staff if commissions and bonuses are not traditionally awarded to non-sales people?

◗ How will this be greeted by those responsible for business development?

More strategic questions are listed in the Appendix at the end of this book.

A company of approximately 40 staff discovered that 60% of their repeat business of £3 million came about as a result of the efforts of one particular middle manager. She was neither paid or rewarded for this behaviour.

At the same company, another senior non-sales manager introduced a friend as a prospective foreign client. On her own initiative she held a preliminary meeting with the head of a US law firm. Once she fully understood his UK business needs, they agreed how her company would present a solution to his team. The Managing Director insisted it was handed over to the Head of Business Development. Threatened by this intrusion into his domain, he decided he 'knew better' and chose to dismiss everything that had been discussed. The proposal that was eventually delivered turned out to be wholly unsuitable. The prospect was shocked to see that it ignored his needs. The manager was furious to see that she had appeared to let him down and been undermined so publicly. She vowed she would never introduce another client again.

It doesn't have to be like this

Since small to medium size companies tend to be relatively flat organisations, they are ideally placed to develop cross-company referral systems. Staff awareness across the range of products, services, and how your company compares to competitors is a prerequisite, as is a culture in which business development isn't seen as the responsibility of a few, but one to which everyone is encouraged and rewarded to make a contribution.

Factors That Determine an Organisation's Referral Gathering Capabilities

Low Level of Referrals	High Level of Referrals
Emphasis on transactions/short term sales	Emphasis on longer term value of client relationship
Inwardly focused company	Client focused company
Closed-book mentality	Commercial transparency with clients
Inconsistent and/ or incongruent corporate values and behaviours	Staff and clients feel alignment with corporate values and behaviours
Selling function monopolised by business development and sales staff	Widespread involvement of staff working closely with sales and business development department
Ad-hoc referrals	Planned referral generation
Weak or non-existent sales processes	Robust sales and business processes

Since a major source of referrals is existing customers, this reinforces the importance of customer focus. Companies that generate a significant proportion of their business through client referral can rightly use this as a key indicator of achieving best practices in customer relationship management (CRM). Conversely, little or no referral activity indicates that key developments in business practices and processes are needed before referral gathering capabilities can be fully exploited.

The behaviour you reward is the behaviour you get - the further staff work away from the bottom line of your business, the more they need to be encouraged to refer potential new clients.

▶ Bonuses, peer recognition and extension of commission to such staff will help motivate individuals and reinforce a referral ready culture. A sustained and long-term approach will help your referral gathering potential soar, particularly if it is fully integrated with 'networking intelligence'.

▶ Attention is needed to ensure that staff who actively identify referral sources share your company's networking and referrals ethos and are confident and able to represent your company's key strengths, benefits and aspirations.

▶ Referrals, and the names of the staff who originated them need to be logged within existing client or prospect databases. It is essential that the staff member be kept in the loop at all times about the progress, not just of the referral but of any subsequent pitch, or business generated because the source may have essential intelligence about the prospective client, and a far deeper understanding of the person than can be gained initially by business development staff.

The pre-existing relationship with the staff source may make the client feel more able to 'talk behind your back' or sound off about any problems to this individual.

- The source can present an informed and united picture of progress, if the client speaks independently to them.

- Acknowledgement of their part in gaining the business is likely to encourage them to seek referrals again, since their trust, integrity and reputation has been enhanced, rather than diminished by the company.

- If business development staff see themselves as competing for the commission, glory, or threatened by the contribution of other staff members, they are likely to act defensively and stifle involvement.

- A cross-functional brainstorm is a great way to kick-start a company referral scheme. Simply start the process by asking questions, such as *"Who do we all know who could become customers of this company?"* and *"Who do we all know who might know other people and organisations that might become our customers?"* See the Appendix for more questions to ignite your brainstorm.

- Regardless of your company size, soliciting referrals from existing clients needs to become a standard part of business processes mapped in at fixed points i.e. at an appropriate interval after purchase, or when clients place repeat orders. Referral generation, however, may well suffer if requests become scripted and impersonal.

- Alternatively or as part of a referral system, referral requests could be left at the discretion of designated 'referral handlers'. Staff members who have demonstrated a high degree of motivation to take on such responsibilities, and who possess trust and rapport with referral givers.

- Records and data logs of referral requests must be made available to all staff involved, to ensure that no client is asked too often by over-enthusiastic staff, or not enough. These logs will also help to ensure proper acknowledgment and progress updates between the all referral stakeholders, as well as offering invaluable sales information to measure the effectiveness of the PeoplePortfolio® Referral Plan. Read on to Chapter two which lists over 100 practical and proven ideas to increase the number and quality of referrals for you and your business.

Chapter 2

Quick Wins

A systematic method for generating referrals becomes a strategic driver within a business. The PeoplePortfolio® Referral Plan described in later chapters and the strategic questions listed at the end of this book will help you develop such a strategy. To gain the most from this book, a strategic approach is recommended.

More referrals, more quickly, is the focus of this chapter. **Here you will find over 100 tactical tips to demonstrate the effectiveness of referrals.** Use these ideas to enhance your strategy. Most people seem to test tactical ideas first to see if they work. Only when they see evidence do they develop a full blown strategy. So here they are, all in one chapter. Each idea has the power to attract highly profitable new business for you - but only if you apply them.

Whilst speaking with and training thousands of sales people and business owners, I have noticed an alarming tendency, whereby for a variety of reasons, seemingly intelligent and professional individuals have a debilitating habit of deciding something won't work for them. They claim to 'know' it won't work, because they believe their situation or particular industry *"doesn't work like that"*.

When you believe something won't work, you will do nothing. This will prove you were correct. It may make you feel good about yourself, but it won't necessarily increase your sales. Or would you rather be right than happy?

You have a choice - you can read these recommendations and decide they won't work for you, or you can ask yourself

"How could I adapt this idea to my own unique situation and use it successfully?

All too often, our behaviour is based on how comfortable we feel about ourselves when we are talking to customers and potential customers. If we don't feel confident about asking for referrals, we won't ask for them as often as we could or should.

Self-employed or running your own micro business? The quality of your work or the level of your skill should be enough - right? Wrong. Too many freelancers, consultants and owner managers 'hate' to sell. They don't want to appear pushy or too 'commercial', so they'd rather not say anything. Even though they may really want or need additional business - the pain of asking is worse than the pain and stress associated with a lack of business.

> **Realise this. Leaving referrals to chance is a crime against your business.**

Develop the Referral Habit

⏵ Each time you receive business from a new customer simply ask them how they found out about you. Go on to explain that a high proportion of your business (say what percentage, if you know it) is by recommendation and referral - indeed the entire success of your business is based on this. If you wish, add *"Because referrals are so important to us, this means we have to work harder for you so you will choose to recommend us in the future."* All this achieves a number of things:

- You collect valuable information that you can use to measure the effectiveness of your business;
- You learn how much business comes in by referral;
- You learn the names of those who are referring you.

This means you will be able to thank that person, which in turn makes it more likely they will continue to recommend you. Why? Because you went to the trouble to thank them. Most of the time people don't thank those who refer business, simply because they don't know who was responsible. As for your new customer it reassures them that they have made a good decision placing their business with you - people who rely on recommendations MUST be good! Finally it is a gentle way of educating your new customer at the outset of your relationship that you take referrals seriously, and at the right time referrals will be offered or asked for. How this is done in a professional and ethical way will be covered in the book.

> *A senior executive at a large multi-national organisation, proudly told me that service levels are SO high, and customers SO happy their customer survey said "92% of customers are prepared to give recommendations." "But how many do?" I asked. "Nothing like that number." Came the reply. Why was this? Because nobody had ever thought to ask them!*

▮ Develop a habit of offering at least four referrals each day. Similarly, ask for four - but not from the same people!

▮ In Rick Crandall's book *1001 Ways to Market Your Services* he tells how Terry Lewis carries 5 paper clips in his pocket every day. Each time he feels one in his pocket he asks the next person he sees for 3 referrals. Once he's received them, he throws away the paper clip. Because this technique helps him keep referrals at the front of his mind, he usually receives 15 new prospects each day.

▮ Scott Kramnick in *Expecting Referrals* discusses his concept of

The Referral Cycle whereby an ever-growing pool of cold, warm and hot prospects is fed at each stage of the cycle; the prospect, pre-appointment contact, the appointment, product delivery and after sales service. Each of these is an opportunity to ask for referrals. He rightly describes the importance of making a 'parallel sale' - selling the contact with the idea of giving referrals, as well as making the product/service sale. He suggests rotating cold, hot and warm calls to referrals to reduce the potential for rejection and help keep the motivation going.

‖ Your habit of reconnecting with others when you DON'T want something is one of the most effective things you can do to stand out in the minds of others.

Communicate The Importance Of Giving And Getting Referrals

‖ *"How's business?"* This is a question I routinely ask members of my audiences. They usually answer *"Fine"*, *"Great"*, *"Fantastic"*, *"Brilliant"*, *"Never been better"*, *"Very buoyant"*, etc. Perhaps they are telling the truth, or maybe a few are putting on a brave face, when in reality business could be better - or even MUCH better! NEVER NEVER answer the question *"How's business?"* in the way I've just described. It may be true. It may make you feel better, by appealing to your ego - but it sends a subconscious signal that you don't want or need additional business. And for anyone who wants to increase their sales - this isn't a good idea. Instead, say something along the following lines; *"Thanks for asking. Business is terrific at the moment. I'm convinced its because we are working really hard to be a company that people choose to recommend. It seems to be working, 65% of our new customers come from referrals."*

Your first thought may be - that's too much of a mouthful. Or it sounds too mechanical for you to use as a response. All too often people ask about your business to be polite, or because they can't think of anything else to say. That's fine. By thanking them for asking, you help them feel good about themselves. Try it. Rehearse it a few times first, you'll feel more comfortable.

▶ We are the gossip species. Human beings talk about each other. It happens anyway. But when we encourage those we know to do it proactively, we dramatically increase the effectiveness of word-of-mouth. If prospects hear about you in a positive way, they may decide to become a customer right away. Although for most, they will just begin to view you more kindly. A combination of positive word-of-mouth from a variety of sources goes a long way towards converting a prospect into a customer.

▶ Assuming you have earned the right, simply contact your closest customers and ask them to talk about your business to people they know. Just being talked about in a positive way will start the referral process for you.

▶ I don't believe in business 'rules' as such. However, when I ask audiences to tell me what they think the first 'rule' of referrals is, it is usually unanimous - *"Ask for referrals"*. I don't agree. Asking for more referrals is the second rule. To me, the first 'rule' for receiving more referrals is to be seen to offer more. **How many referrals have you and your colleagues provided to your contacts and customers in the past week, month, year?** It's unrealistic to expect to receive referrals if you don't give them. By offering high quality referrals to your own contacts, a proportion will look for referrals on your behalf too.

- The next time a customer gives a compliment say "*Thank you. Would you be prepared to put that into writing?*" They may think you were joking, so gently say "*I'm serious. It would mean a lot to me. I am always looking for written testimonials from delighted customers.*" For more information on how to make even more of testimonials see Chapter 5.

Optimise Your Referral Gathering Capabilities

- How many people work for your company? "*About half*" is the wrong answer! What if everyone within your company learned to understand why it was so important to say this to everyone who asked about the business? Think how powerful that could be.

- Brainstorm the possible sources of referrals within your company. Get everyone together (including non-sales staff) to discuss who you all know from previous employment, highly regarded suppliers, friends and relatives. **How many could and would suggest people and organisations they know who could become new customers?** All too often we overlook our colleagues and the people closest to us as potential sources of referrals.

- Non-sales (especially sales support) staff are an under-utilised sales resource in most companies. All too often they complain they don't receive any commission or financial benefits for helping the sales people earn their high bonuses. Many of these people are very knowledgeable about your business, they could be influential advocates for you. Motivate them to attract customers out of business hours by printing business cards for staff who are interested. Invite them to hand out these cards to those they identify as prospects. Then offer a commission or, if that's not possible, a non-financial perk for each piece of business from a caller mentioning their name.

- Have a 'Referral of the Month' competition with all your colleagues. This increases the likelihood that they will think more about referrals on a daily basis. Ensure the scheme is structured to enhance and NOT harm a sense of teamwork.

- Strategically target 'better' clients. This has the effect of attracting referrals from even higher profile clients in the future.

- If your current offer does not lead to repeat business, what can you add to your product/service offering that will?

- If you work within a large organisation, make it a priority to get to know colleagues in other parts of the business. You can increase the number and quality of 'cross referrals' if you find out what business they are looking for, and educate them to spot the types of opportunity you are most interested in.

> *I once spoke at a conference for a global organisation that included an exhibition. There was a booth for every department within the company. Each department competed for prizes to produce the most informative and interactive exhibit. The result? The best way they had ever educated everyone within the company to more fully understand the focus, needs and expertise of their colleagues. For the first time, everyone had a clear idea of how they could sell in solutions from other parts of the business to their existing client base. The number of cross referrals soared.*

- Hire high-calibre people with lots of contacts.

- If you are looking to recruit more high calibre people to your company, encourage (even financially reward) your existing staff to recommend the best people they know. Be proactive about it. Your staff will feel they are being listened to.

⮕ What perceptions are staff creating by the way they describe the company to the people they meet out of work hours? If they feel unappreciated or mistreated they will share it with whoever will listen. So, 1) treat your people well 2) help them realise how fundamentally important it is to the future success of the business (and their jobs) for them to talk well of the business 'behind your back'. They have a crucial role to play to help generate positive word-of-mouth within their circle of friends and contacts. What do staff say when asked "What does your company do?" What would you prefer them to say? Perhaps you and your staff could formulate a better response. Work together to come up with a few options that staff would be willing to use.

⮕ Put up a sign in your office, waiting room or store saying *"We Appreciate Referrals - Please Tell Your Friends and Business Associates About Us."* If you're a new business, tell your customers *"We are a New Business - Please Recommend Us"*.

⮕ Include similar notices when you send out invoices. Put them on your brochures, web site, company vehicles, your business cards.

⮕ Print a request for referrals on the back of your order forms or business reply envelopes.

⮕ If you publish a company report, it will be read by those most interested in your business - especially shareholders who have a vested interest in your success. Include a section clearly defining the profiles of your preferred customers. Provide details of a specific person for readers to contact with the names of people they can refer to your company.

▮ Include something similar in your newsletters, staff journals, customer magazines and website. It costs so little to do - yet the payback can be high.

Align Yourself With Others

▮ Identify people in a complementary business. Refer business to each other. Think laterally.

▮ Create affinity groups. Membership organisations are often strapped for cash and are keen to offer their members preferential terms on a number of services. Provide a genuine good deal to members. This is great for the organisation, because they are seen to offer higher value to members at no cost to them. Perhaps you would be able to offer a small commission to the organisation for each sale. Many not-for-profit organisations are desperate to find ways to maintain or increase their membership subscriptions - so help them. Doing so is a great way to increase your own sales volumes 'privately', so you are not seen to openly discount your products and services which may undermine their perceived value or brand position. Members could be a healthy source of new referrals, more than making up for lower profits per initial sale.

▮ Become an expert on where to get the best deals on a wide variety of products and services. And educate your best contacts to call you whenever they are thinking of making a significant purchase, so you can help them find the best deal. This avoids the problem of calling them on a regular basis when you haven't got anything specific to offer them. When they are motivated to re-connect with you, referrals will be easier to ask for.

‣ Assemble on one sheet of paper a list of your preferred suppliers and professionals. Put your name at the top and entitle it [Your Name] Recommends... And send it out to the people in your network. You may be able to persuade those on the list to offer a preferential rate to anyone who mentions your name when they call.

‣ If you are an estate agent/realtor - why not put together a list of local service providers, who you can confidently recommend to new people to your area. Brainstorm the services needed. Include builders, decorators, plumbers, cleaners, gardeners, babysitters and local organisations. Its added value for clients and potentially increased income for you, if these suppliers agree to pay you a finders fee for each piece of business that comes their way.

‣ As a professional speaker on the subject of networking and referrals, giving and receiving referrals is an essential element of my own business. After I have worked with a client, they would frequently tell me they were looking for another speaker for their next meeting. Who would I recommend? These days I'm more proactive. I say to clients *If you ever need high-calibre speakers or trainers - ask me. I can probably help.* As someone they have come to trust, a high proportion of people take me up on it. I recommend speakers I know will deliver a great result. The client can be confident they have someone suitable. I've helped the client, so I've been more valuable. The speaker gets the extra business. It's a service to the client and to my most trusted speaker colleagues. And they are more likely to recommend me to their clients. Everyone is happy.

‣ Offer to carry around 6 or so business cards or brochures for each of your closest business friends. When an opportunity presents itself for one of these contacts, hand one out. Obviously, encourage them to do the same for you.

◗ In *Getting Everything You Can Out Of All You've Got* Jay Abraham includes this referral idea; a catering business that offers a special service for food allergy sufferers and a new line of food products, instigated a referral programme encouraging friends and fellow sufferers to subscribe to the meals service or request the foods at their stores. The store products included on-pack ads to cross-sell the meals service. Comment; Clearly defined groups such as food allergy sufferers in this case are a great way to gain access to larger groups of customers. Which groups already service your target customers? If none exist, it might be worth creating them yourself. When members derive value from being a member, others with similar needs will find you, especially if you encourage them to provide you with referrals!

Generate More Business From Existing Customers

◗ Get in touch with every previous customer or client (but only those who you would want to work with again!), assuming you did a competent job, it's safe to predict that you would end up with profitable new business. Forgetting clients you have worked with in the past is a costly mistake to any sales person or business owner. Maintain your relationship with all your clients and customers. Why? Previous happy customers are always the easiest people to sell to. They know and trust you. Working again for past clients is more profitable than constantly spending time and money to find new clients. Known as 'top of the mind' marketing - you will find a significant amount of repeat business will come your way. Inexperienced business people tell me they don't maintain contact because they think they will be seen as a nuisance and don't want to be seen to pester anyone. If your approach is one of helping your clients, they will not think of you as a nuisance when you contact them.

▶ Put together a list of your largest or best customers. How did they become customers? Wherever possible, track each one back to the source. If you don't know, find out. Customers who came to you as a referral are prime candidates for the following approach. Ask in person or write a letter along the following lines

"You are one of our most valued customers. Recently we decided to find out how you became one of our customers/clients. It appears we were recommended by .... Our research has found that x% of our business is by recommendation. Hopefully this means we are doing something right! Referrals are very important to the future success of our company. This means we have to remain committed to offering a high level of service to our existing customers.

Seeing as you decided to do business with us following a recommendation, who do you know who might also benefit from working with us?" Perhaps we can have a discussion at a convenient time to explore this further. I will give you a call."

Make this letter as tangible as possible - its worth finding out what proportion of your business is by referral. Use the figures. It will reinforce the perception in the mind of your customers that they do business with a high quality company. This will further increase your chances of referrals. It's essential that you follow it up with a phone call or face-to-face meeting, to gather the names of people you are given. Exactly how to do this is covered in Chapter 4.

▶ Develop the habit of contacting your customers at times when you do not want anything. Better yet, offering business opportunities to them is a pretty good start.

▶ When you go into every job or contract with the mindset of *"What can I do to ensure my client is so delighted with our work they will want to offer referrals?"* You will.

◗ Test and measure your effectiveness at gathering referrals with every new customer from now on.

◗ Many of your best customers and most ardent supporters won't give you referrals unless you remind them.

◗ People who have offered you written testimonials are the most likely to offer you referrals. Go to them first. Ask who they think you should be talking to?

◗ Look at ways you can help your clients make more money for themselves. Re-read this tip - think about it deeply. Nothing will help you more to grow your business if you become known as someone who seeks to help others grow theirs.

◗ Especially go back to customers who have been motivated to give you referrals in the past. They are your biggest fans. As long as you have continued to offer a good service, it's highly likely they will offer more. However, what stops most people is feeling uncomfortable about asking again. They don't want to be a nuisance - or be seen to 'push their luck'. This need not be the case.

◗ Jay Abraham cites these two examples; 1) New members at a health club have to make a commitment to use the club and set personal health goals. When they reach those goals, they are asked to write a personal letter of recommendation to their friends. 50% of new members agree to do so.

2) A stockbroker found that referrals were rarely offered because clients were afraid of feeling responsible if their friends investments failed. To address this he told existing clients that his job was to find the best investments for them. If he had to

spend a high proportion of his time looking for new clients he would not be able to devote as much time finding the best investments for THEM. He then asked "What would you prefer me to do?" The quality of his referrals improved dramatically.

▶ Complaining customers are potential sources of many referrals. Seriously. If you are seen to move heaven and earth to sort out their problems, some will be so pleased that they may want to tell their contacts about what you did for them. Others, however may never appreciate you! Who knows, you may reach a situation where you will be able to 'fire' your most troublesome customers.

Solicitation Tactics

▶ Frank Furness is a sales trainer in the financial services market. He is successful at receiving referrals. While working with a particular off-shore company on the island of Jersey, three different people told him the name of someone he should contact. But each person said *"Please don't mention my name - because he's such a bastard."* . But Frank decided to call him. After introducing himself he said *"Three people have independently told me to call you. But all three said "Don't mention my name because you're such a bastard? I'm intrigued - are you?"* The guy burst out laughing and invited him in for a meeting. He was a direct person and appreciated Frank's approach. Do you have the nerve to try this?

▶ Here's a sales script for gathering referrals developed by author and speaker Peter Thomson. When you know a client has been particularly happy with your products or service, generate the following conversation:

Q. *"How long have you been in your line of business?"*

Then add

Q. *"I suppose you've met lots of other people in your business over those years - haven't you?"* The "haven't you" is important because it gets the person to mentally say "Yes" to themselves. It's called a 'yes tag' question. Go on by saying

Q. *"If I asked you to write down the names - you could, couldn't you? When you say this, shrug your shoulders and almost throw away the - "you could, couldn't you?"* It's another 'yes tag' question.Then ask

Q. *"Can I ask your advice?"*

Q. *"Which of those people should I contact first to do some work with them?"*

Practice it with a friend or colleague until you become comfortable with the script.

⮕ This is a very powerful question to ask a new customer face-to-face *"What is the most important thing you expect from your [name of your profession]for you to choose to recommend me to your friends and colleagues?"* Say this with absolute sincerity, look into their eyes and wait. Deliver on what they say. You'll get lots more referrals.

⮕ Referrals author and trainer Mark Sheer, recommends sending out letters which begin; *"I am looking to expand my business. I need your help. Who do you know who..."* He believes this wording is crucial for success and urges you not to change or 'improve' it in any way. Attached to the letter is a customer profile - one sheet of paper giving as much detail of exactly who you are looking to do business with.

⮕ A financial advisor once took me aside to share the following story. He'd attended a business seminar and got on particularly well with the other attendees, who were predominantly the owners of small businesses and people most in need of his services. He followed up the seminar with a letter and then a phone call. When he spoke to these people on the phone they were unfriendly, even cool towards him. He sensed he'd made a big mistake, but couldn't figure out what he had done wrong. The content of his letter provided the answer. He wrote *"It was wonderful to meet you at the seminar. As you know I am a financial advisor. If I can ever help you with your pensions or insurance, please contact me. I will call you in the next week."* When he called, everyone knew that they were now prospects! I suggested a different approach. In the future, write your letter as follows; *"It was great to meet you etc."* Then add *"As a financial advisor, I meet high level people from all walks of life, and from different industries and businesses. Let me know how I could identify potential customers for your business. Please give this some thought. I will call you in a week to discuss it further."* Your follow up call will almost certainly be met with more enthusiasm.

▮▶ When asking for referrals Bill Cates uses this approach: With a twinkle in the eye he says *"I'd like you to give me 100 names..."* Then he laughs. *"OK, how about two or three?"* This way you get more than one.

▮▶ When Burt Dubin asks for referrals he uses the phrase *"If you were me, who would you call next?"* He then says *"Why did you choose him or her?"* He writes down and later uses what is said.

▮▶ One of the most powerful questions in business is *"How would I recognize a good business referral for you?"*

▮▶ Write by letter or email all of your friends, colleagues, and customers asking for the necessary information to identify customers and clients for them. Be sure to include individuals who have offered referrals to you in the past. Offer other types of help. If you can, use a real example of how you discovered a friend or colleague needed help you could have offered, if only you had known in time. Implore your contacts to request the help they need. Then help them.

◗ Offer a referral in the PS of letters you send out, specific to the needs of that person. Add that referrals are so valuable to the success of your own business, that you make a point of offering referrals as often as you can. Include the fact that you can personally vouch for the quality of that person's work and professionalism.

◗ A tip from financial advisor Morwenna Edwards. When you give out your business card, gently touch their lower arm and say *"Don't just give anyone my telephone number unless they promise to mention your name. When they call, they won't be a stranger"*.

◗ Which of your delighted customers would be prepared to send an introductory letter on your behalf to their contact list? You write it with their collaboration, print it onto their stationery, they sign it and you pay the postage.

◗ If you can, fix up a lunch appointment with the sole aim of brainstorming opportunities for them, not you. During your meeting include the phrase *"I realise just how important referrals are to the success of any business - they're certainly crucial to my own. How can I find ways to deliver quality referrals to you."* Then leave it at that. Proactively find referrals and opportunities for this person. Do not ask for referrals - yet. Focus on being of value to that person. Once you have proved yourself, then and only then should you broach the subject of referrals. Do NOT ask that person for their business. Simply educate this person about who you look for as a client. And who you choose not to work with (and why). See Chapter 4 for detailed information on 'asking for referrals'.

▶ In SalesDoctor magazine, a reader wrote; *"My brother has an insurance agency that sells all types of insurance. Customers visit his office to pay their premiums all the time. In order to get referrals from his regular customers, he has a small sign on everyone's desk that states: FREE MUG, ASK HOW. Because the office staff are busy and forget to ask for referrals, the sign encourages customers to enquire about the mugs. The staff member states that, in exchange for a mug, the company wants 3 referrals with phone numbers and addresses. 85% of the people give this information to get a mug, and many give more names to earn a set of mugs. The cost of the program is about $1.00 per mug, with an average return of $35.00 per sale. This has been a big success for the agency."*

Recognise The Negotiable Value Of Referrals

▶ Freelancers and consultants will know that some clients have a habit of asking for a 'deal' - better known as a discount! You may agree a discount if you want or need the project. Rather than simply saying *"Yes"*, try *"I would be prepared to offer you a discount - this time* (its important to include this as it sends a signal that you don't always agree to offer one.) Then add *"...on condition you provide me with two high quality referrals and a written testimonial, following the completion of this project. Of course, I wouldn't expect you to do this unless you were totally satisfied with my work."* If the client agrees (most fair minded people will) confirm this agreement in writing as a follow up. When you eventually ask for referrals, it won't come as a surprise to them. You've been able to save face, they get a better deal and you earn the right to expect referrals and a written testimonial. Not bad - you were going to ask for them anyway!

❯ A beauty salon in the historic city of Bath published a promotional flyer that said *"No tips. We are always looking for clients to be so pleased with our service that you recommend us to your family, friends and colleagues instead."* They know that referrals are far more valuable than a tip. Few businesses ever think of telling their customers that they actually want referrals. By gently alluding to the fact that they aim to deliver particularly high levels of service, the salon helps its customers realise how good the service is. Letting customers 'off the hook' from paying the tip also has the effect of reinforcing a positive feeling about the salon, therefore increasing the chance that the customer will indeed speak well of the salon to her friends. A win-win for the customer and for the salon.

❯ Build referrals into your client contracts. *"If we take you on as a client and you are delighted with our service, you agree to write 3 letters of recommendation to people who you believe would be most interested in our services."* This can appear harsh, but if you are genuinely selective about the clients you take on, this approach can help you weed out clients you don't want.

❯ Another idea from Jay Abraham; A company selling building plots specified that before a potential buyer could write a cheque, they would not be accepted as a customer unless they provided 5 referrals too. They sold 113 plots in 120 days.

Incentivise Referral Giving

❯ The best word-of-mouth promotions bring in new customers, whilst simultaneously helping those who refer the business to look good to those they recommend. Perhaps you could offer specially printed coupons, or better still - certificates that can look more impressive - to your best customers. They could offer a discount or a free gift. Then leave a space for the customer's name. The discount or free gift is from them and not you. They become referrals, rather than just pieces of paper, when the customer passes them on to their contacts

most likely to take up the offer. Important: Include a time limit for the offer. When the coupon/certificate is redeemed, send a small gift (if appropriate) and a personal hand-written thank you note to the person whose name is on the coupon, to tell them who had taken it up. This demonstrates a high degree of customer care, and more importantly, by showing appreciation, you increase the likelihood that they will direct more business your way. Rewarding a behaviour encourages people to repeat it!

A hairdresser gave out certificates to existing customers offering a free bottle of shampoo to any friends who had their hair cut within the next month. The customer could request as many certificates as they liked. Each one included the customer's name and said "Have your hair cut at [name of salon] before [date] and you will receive a free [size]ml bottle of [brand name] shampoo courtesy of [customer name]. When each certificate was redeemed, the person who's name appeared on the certificate was also given a free bottle of shampoo. A low cost promotion that brought in profitable new clients.

The Institute of Directors in the UK offers a variety of gifts including a case of Champagne to members who refer other company directors to join the organisation. Just a thought; I was to MC a large awards dinner for one of my clients. For the past year, they had devoted an enormous amount of time, energy and money to convey the importance of values within the organisation. I don't have anything against alcohol but quietly asked the MD what the booze they were offering to reward staff with could be saying about the values of the company. This had never occurred to him. They changed the prizes.

> *Amazon.com the on-line book retailer pioneered 'affiliate programmes'. These are fast becoming a major new sales channel on the internet. How does it work? On your own website you might recommend a book (or any other product). If your visitor wants to know more about it, they simply click a link which takes them to the website where you can buy it. Why would you want to send a visitor to another site? Amazon pays a commission on each product you help them sell. There's no cost to Amazon, your site is seen to offer a better service to visitors, and you make money. Some affiliate programmes pay anything from 8-20% on each sale. It's done automatically.*

More and more organisations have woken up to the profit potential of such on-line referrals. See Chapter 9. For the most up-to-date details of organisations that offer affiliate programmes visit www.RoySpeaks.com/refer.htm

▮ This arrived from Amazon.co.uk by email. *"Refer-A-Friend". If you have friends or relatives who haven't yet become Amazon customers, give us their names and email addresses and we'll send them £5 each in your name. And as a way of saying thanks, we'll send you a £5 gift certificate for every one of them that becomes an Amazon.co.uk customer."* They then included a special internet link to take you to a form to fill in the names and contact details of your friends. Amazon have realised that the longer term value of every new customer is worth far more to them than any initial discounts and gifts they offer. Once they attract a new customer, their job is to impress them so much with their service, no customer would ever think to order their books (or whatever else they decide to sell) from anywhere else. Other on-line booksellers now offer similar deals.

▶ After a few weeks being a member of WeightWatchers® (after years of battling with a weight problem, it has worked fantastically.) I received a "friends" leaflet. For each friend or partner introduced, I was offered a discount on products, while the referral receives free registration. This is a good example of both parties benefiting. The offer also had a time limit to encourage members to do it instantly. Without the time limit, most people would leave it to some other time and then probably forget.

▶ The late Howard Shenson in his book *Shenson On Consulting* stresses the importance of maintaining the gifts you choose to demonstrate your appreciation for referrals. There's no point offering a gift for the first referral, then nothing for the second or third. The referral giver may interpret this as a sign of unappreciation or being taken for granted.

▶ If paying a commission to those who refer business to you is unpalatable, for each new customer they refer offer to make a donation to your favourite charity or theirs.

> *The movie industry learned decades ago that a cinemagoer needs to see a positive message about a particular film at least seven times before they decide to go to see it. The industry relies heavily on what reviewers say. The better the reputation of the reviewer, the higher the credibility of the review and its ability to persuade you to pay to see the film. However, we listen the most to the views of our closest friends and colleagues. What the public says about a movie will make or break it. It's the same for your business. You can let it happen naturally or you can take a proactive approach.*

Build Your Profile And They Will Come

▶ Identify the most influential individuals within your target markets. Who do your prospective customers listen to and trust?

▶ Invest your time and energy getting to know these people. They have enormous power. They can help you, if you deserve to be helped.

▶ What customers and prospects say about you or your company 'Behind your back', will have a massive impact on your success at attracting referral business. You MUST know. Ask friends, colleagues and customers what people say about your company. Convince them that you really want to know - good, bad and indifferent. Build up a picture of how others perceive you. Request negative comments especially because these can seriously undermine your efforts to increase referrals.

▶ Plan and execute a "Behind Your Back" campaign. (See Chapter 6) Your aim is to motivate the maximum number of people to speak positively about you and/or your business to everyone they know, as often as possible, in order to generate new sales. Valuable referrals will come from individuals who do not know you personally, or have never actually conducted business with you. They will refer their contacts if they hear enough positive reports about you from high credibility sources. These include; local, regional and national newspapers, magazines, newsletters, books, websites, radio and TV programmes. Positive messages can by BY you, or ABOUT you.

▶ By you; Send letters to editors or write articles in selected newspapers and general or industry specific magazines. This includes existing client newsletters.

▮▶ About you; Be featured as an interviewee in newspapers, magazines, newsletters, websites, radio and TV programmes. Be the subject of written, audio or video testimonials from your most satisfied clients.

During an in-house seminar, I encouraged staff to share what they believed was said behind their back. It was like pulling teeth. No one wanted to say anything, until one brave soul said "We have a reputation for being bad payers. We take forever to pay our suppliers' invoices. This makes it difficult to attract the best contractors, who in turn influence the perception our clients have of the quality of our work." Progress! But it was short lived. A company director jumped in to say "That is not a problem." End of subject. However, a couple of weeks later I spoke at a conference. During coffee I got into conversation with two delegates - both were consultants in the same industry as my client. I told them that I'd just worked with a really nice bunch of people and named the company. With no prompting from me they both said "I wouldn't touch them. They don't pay." I fed this back, but was not hopeful it would make a difference. The finance department was obviously doing a great job managing the companies' cash flow, but at what price to the business?

What people say behind your back is VERY powerful.

▮▶ Be clear about what you would like people to say about you. What elements of your company service and behaviour do you and your colleagues need to improve, in order to deserve such plaudits? Ask your clients for this information.

▶ Circulate case studies and stories so others speak positively about you and your business. To increase the likelihood of this happening - consistently deliver outstanding products and services. Nothing will replace this.

▶ Bad news can travel quickly - you need to be aware of any negativity that is being circulated about you. Develop your own unofficial intelligence network of contacts to keep their ears to the ground for you. Perhaps competitors are spreading malicious rumours about you - you need to know as early as possible so you can counter them. Look after your own contacts in the same way.

▶ Communicate improvements back to your customers by explaining that you had heard about the problems/issues and how they have been rectified. For anything that needs additional time, offer an idea of how long it will take before they notice an improvement. Make sure you fulfil your promise.

▶ To reach those who don't talk about you because they don't know you yet, there are a number of strategies open to you. Being written about in the trade press of your target market is more straight-forward than you may believe - but only if you understand how it really works. You don't need a large PR budget to get results, although it has to be said that Rapid Results they are not. It takes time, but is worth it.

Speaker coach Burt Dubin describes referrals as *"The oxygen that fuels my business."* Could you adopt this mindset too?

⏵ Publish your own newsletter or magazine and include a *"Thank You"* page or column. Briefly describe the circumstances surrounding each referral and credit the person you made it all possible. Public thanks in this way serves a number of purposes;

- it sends a signal to other customers that you reward referrals with recognition.
- The person who offered the referral will feel appreciated.
- And you are providing much needed 'news' for your publication.

Check beforehand that the person does not mind being identified in this way. Once he/she has given the go ahead ask for a photo. Or better still, commission a photographer to visit the customer at their place of work or take the shot yourself. It's a perfect opportunity to re-connect. Offer to send multiple copies of the publication to the referrer if they wish to circulate it to their contacts.

⏵ Find someone to record an interview with you. High quality audio and video recording and editing equipment is now so inexpensive, this is feasible for most businesses. Create an audio or video cassette tape. It creates a sense of who you are. Give copies to interested clients. Encourage your customers/fans to hand them out to their contacts. Keep them supplied with tapes.

⏵ Master the art of public speaking. Initially, join Toastmasters International or enrol on a Dale Carnegie speaking course. You'll find the nearest ones in the phone book. Speaking in public is the second biggest fear after death itself, for the majority of the population. But it's a skill that can be learned. These organisations will show you how to structure a talk, help you appear more confident (even if you're not) and engage an audience with a higher degree of skill. Professional speakers will tell you that everyone gets butterflies in the stomach - competent speakers have merely found a way to get them to fly in formation! (see Chapter 7)

▶ Conduct a survey. Use this as a reason to contact your customers and then re-visit them with the findings. Publish the information to gain media exposure.

▶ How can you give your clients and contacts free publicity? So long as it's good publicity, they will almost certainly appreciate it - but check first.

▶ Mention your contacts in the articles you write and wherever possible include their contact details in a "breakout box" at the end.

▶ Develop talkability. What stands you out from your competitors? What makes you worth being talked about? Become a pace-setter. Be newsworthy.

Get Connected

▶ Join a referral club. People either love or hate them. BNI (Business Network International) is one of the better-known and has become global in nature, although some are better organised than others. Each chapter only allows one representative company from each industry, to ensure that members don't end up fighting for the same business opportunities. Meetings are run using a format developed by its founder, Ivan Misner PhD in 1985. Feedback from a small number of British people who have attended a BNI meeting includes the comment *"The format is inflexible. It doesn't work in this country."* But for most attendees it does deliver new business. One more point - meetings take place at 7am. Therefore, only the most motivated tend to go! Every referral given and received is logged and quantified. Visit www.BNI.com for details of your nearest chapter.

◗ If more conventional referral (or leads) clubs do not exist in your area - start your own, or a new BNI Chapter.

◗ Other unofficial referral clubs include the secretive Masonic Lodges. To join, you have to be referred! Visit www.RoySpeaks.com/refer.htm for a growing list of other business network groups. Please supply those you belong to.

◗ Which customers would be prepared to take you along to their trade association meetings for the purpose of introducing and endorsing you to their colleagues and peers?

◗ Get involved in local community organisations and charitable projects. Generally speaking, highly successful people join them as their way of 'giving something back'. Contribute. Don't join just to use the members for your own selfish purposes. You WILL be found out. Choose to be more than a name on their notepaper.

◗ As part of this 'contribution marketing', in every locality there are a huge range of meetings covering every interest imaginable. There are business, political, hobby, health, voluntary and charity meetings. Knowing who meets where and when can be invaluable for identifying groups of potential customers. As part of this research, develop a comprehensive list of every business and social group that meets locally and regionally. Don't forget ethnic and women/male groups. Ask people you already know for their ideas. When you've finished compiling the list (together with contact names and phone numbers), circulate a copy or post it on your website, and inform those who helped you put it together. Position it as a service to the community. Include the phrase at the bottom *"If you know of any other group that has been omitted from this list, please contact me."* If space and time permits, contact and invite the organisers of each group to provide you with details of who they would welcome as future members/attendees, as well as times and venues of their meetings. Include this information on your website if you have one. It personalises a site and demonstrates to non-local visitors that your organisation has a sense of community.

I) Get out more. A simple tip - yet too many people these days think they are 'too busy' to get 'belly to belly' with existing customers and new contacts. Make it a priority by building at least one networking event or lunch appointment into your weekly calendar - and go.

Generate Referrals Via Events And Exhibitions

I) Hold a series or one-off events. Encourage your customers and suppliers to bring along their own favoured customers and suppliers. You'll enlarge your own base of contacts, and probably meet more individuals with similar beliefs and values. Do not use the situation to sell to them. It seriously undermines your credibility. Develop the relationship first to increase the trust. Make those who invite their colleagues look good - publicly thank and acknowledge them for bringing everyone together. You are simply the catalyst. A small proportion of the guests could become customers, but that's not the aim. Tapping into THEIR network of contacts is potentially far more valuable to you.

II) Organise training sessions for your staff and invite clients to attend free of charge. Even encourage them to invite others. This need not cost much more than the cost of the training. Everyone gets a shared experience, as well as new and potentially valuable skills and knowledge. Following the training session, include a buffet meal to encourage delegates to mingle and get to know each other better. It makes the company look good whilst simultaneously offering an opportunity to meet new people. It also has the potential to more than double the size of the training session.

II) Advisory boards or customer focus groups in the pharmaceutical industry are a common way of generating high-level feedback and insight. How could you benefit from better, more up-to-date information and knowledge? Create your own advisory boards by inviting key people to be a part of them. Conversely, offer to be a member of advisory boards for others.

II) Put together a group of like-minded individuals (including your keenest supporters) especially those from different, non-competing businesses, to discuss opportunities for one another. Provide a couple of bottles of wine and food, if appropriate, and encourage the group to help each other. Ensure that everyone is seen to gain something of value from each meeting. For subsequent meetings, encourage members of the group to invite new high-calibre contacts. My own group *"The Good Guys"* (it includes male and female members) may not meet that often but by keeping connected via email, results have been spectacular.

II) Howard Shenson recalls a seasoned professional, who offers twice yearly all-expenses paid weekends at resorts, hunting or ski lodges for his most valued clients and referral sources. The weekends offer invaluable opportunities for those attending to get to know each other and includes business workshops where the consultant offers his latest thinking on a variety of topics. (No doubt offering a tax break on the event too!).

⏵ Send savvy people to events on your behalf. Their job is to identify key people, make contact with them and speak highly of you or your organisation in the ways you have mutually agreed.

⏵ Perhaps some customers would be willing to hold a party or drinks reception in your honour. They would invite key influencers, colleagues and prospects for you. They get the credit for the party - you pay for it.

⏵ Compile a high quality presentation folder containing all your brochures, business cards and best testimonial letters. Carry it with you always. Include the business cards and promotional material of those you choose to refer.

⏵ Think ahead if you are going to be attending events, exhibitions, seminars. Find out if your contacts and customers are going to be there - send a note suggesting that you meet up.

Keep Existing And Potential Referral Sources In The Loop

⏵ Send your in-house newsletter to customers, especially those who refer you.

⏵ Write by hand, or (this won't appeal to everyone) send a specially printed postcard to everyone who refers business to you. Leave a space for their name - then print *"Thank you for referring .... to us as a patient/client. We deeply appreciate your support. You can be assured we will do everything we can to deliver the best possible service to this person."* Such a note will go a long way towards reassuring the referrer that they did the right thing to refer business to you. And by telling them that you will look after the customer in this way, they will feel even better about doing so and, more importantly, they'll be more inclined to refer more people in the future.

▮▶ Being photographed with your customers is always a smart move. Sending the photos on to them is a great way to reconnect.

▮▶ Offer to take to lunch the person who gave you a referral, as well as the one being referred.

▮▶ To thank someone for a referral send a letter, note or email along the following lines attributed to Jim Rhode author of *10 Secrets of Marketing Success "Referrals like yours are the nicest compliment we can receive. We appreciate your confidence in us. Through referrals by good clients like you, we have created a positive work environment. A thank you hardly seems enough for your consideration and trust. Thank you again for your confidence."*

▮▶ When you send a hand-written thank you note, why not enclose a lottery ticket? Don't forget to tell them is theirs.

Stay Connected

▮▶ The time to seek referrals is when you don't need them, NOT when business is 'flat'. So it pays to stay connected to your potential referral sources.

▮▶ Embrace the concept of 'The Rule of Four'. Re-connect every day with at least four people (customers, clients, prospects and friends) you haven't seen or spoken to in a while. You can do so by phone, fax, letter, handwritten note, email or face-to-face.

▮▶ Here's another variation by author Andrea Neirenberg. She has what she calls her 'Power of Three Note Plan'. Everyday she writes three handwritten notes; one to a prospect, one to a client, and one to a friend. At the end of each week, by investing about 12 minutes a day, she's made 15 connections and at the end of the year, over 750 people will have received her goodwill notes. Its good for her business. And could do the same for yours.

▮▶ Send out personal handwritten notes to your clients and contacts EVERY day. How many do you receive? Possibly only a few. Here are the possible reasons

- you don't do anything worthy of a thank you!
- people you know are too busy to send them or
- they don't realise just how powerful this simple technique can be to forge a positive place in other people's lives. Think back to the time when you received one - how did it make you feel? Probably pretty good.

Use postcards, greetings cards, compliment slips, your company letter heading or create your own postcards and greetings cards solely to say thank you. I use printed plain flat cards with my contact details A5 size (21x14.4cm or 81/4" x 511/16"). You might decide to include a small photo of yourself on each one. It helps people remember who you are.

▮▶ Handwritten notes on or attached to catalogues, brochures, and invoices personalise the material you send out. It takes moments to do and customers appreciate your attention.

⏺ From the book *Million-Dollar Prospecting Techniques*. Print a note pad with your name and contact details at the bottom of each page. At the top, use a small logo and your result producing slogan. Include your photograph. Ensure that there is a great deal of space for people to write. Send these notepads to everyone you can think of. Indeed send two each so they can pass one on to their friends or colleagues. You will be a constant reminder to them. This will help to ensure that you are at the front of their mind when a possible opportunity for you comes up.

⏺ Don't be a 'know all'. Not knowing the answer to every one of your customer's questions is OK. (So long as it's not a habit) It actually gives you the perfect reason to get in touch with them again, in order to strengthen your relationship and increase the likelihood of referrals.

⏺ If you spot something in the paper your contacts may be interested in - send it to them. Video a TV programme that may be of interest, check if they saw it, if not, send them the tape.

⏺ Encourage your customers to talk about their business. Care about their business. Listen attentively. Some customers won't want a relationship. Accept this. However, sometimes people just want a shoulder to cry on. Be there for your best customers.

There are too many ideas listed in this chapter to try them all at once. Be selective. Choose the ones that are most likely to deliver rapid results for you. As you'll discover, if you experiment with just some of them, your confidence will increase. This will mean you are more likely to try more in the future. So, try a few now and then make an appointment in your diary to read this book again (or just this chapter) in two or three months - and again three months after that. Your confidence and mindset will have changed. What you may have skipped past during the first reading is more likely to jump out at you a second or third time around as a viable approach for your business.

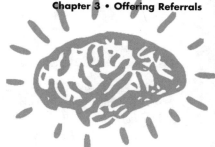

Chapter 3

Your PeoplePortfolio® Referral Plan

Part 1 - Offering Referrals

So many young, ambitious, highly motivated salespeople simply want to go out and make the next sale. They are FOCUSED!!!! All they work for is the commission to pay for that sports car and the swanky house they have photographs of stuck inside their goal planner or on the desk in front of them. They don't have the time to help others. They are FOCUSED!!!! They are convinced that every minute they help someone else, they lose a minute towards making their next sale. *"Time is money, you know!"*

So, there's no time to help others. And as for ASKING for help. Forget it. These highly motivated FOCUSED salespeople don't need it. 'Everybody knows - asking for help is for the desperate or the weak.' **They may be FOCUSED ...but they're looking at the wrong pictures.**

Having goals is great. I fully recommend it. But if you can't or won't offer and accept help from people you know, like, trust and value, you are practically guaranteed to remain an average, or below-average salesperson or business owner. **Learning to be truly inter-dependent is a key success skill.**

For some, the idea of offering referrals and help with no promise of a return, will continue to stick in their throat.

> *I gave over £10,000 worth of referrals to someone. She thanked me. But I never saw any evidence that she gave opportunities to others (none came my way either). One day she made a comment about how 'yukky' she felt about giving referrals. She smiled and shuddered and hasn't received another referral from me since. Colleagues have commented that they have stopped offering opportunities to her too. I hadn't said a word.*

Should an offer of help or referrals be conditional of a return favour? Not at all. However, people who receive the most referrals over a long time tend to have an 'Abundance Mentality' rather than a 'Scarcity Mentality' as defined by Stephen Covey, author of *The Seven Habits of Highly Effective People*. People with an abundance mentality realise *"the good that goes around, comes around"*. They know that the world is big enough for others to be successful too. Someone with a scarcity mentality is usually afraid of losing something. They've been let down, swindled or abused in the past. They are determined they will never get 'taken' again. But that same fear can stifle, paralyse or rob you of better results in your life. If you tend to suffer from a scarcity mentality, try to figure out why you think and behave that way. Learn to be a little more trusting of others. Accept that some will let you down occasionally. Most won't.

You might be thinking *"But I really don't have the time to run around for other people all the time."* Helping people isn't the same as being a 'doormat', always at the beck and call of everyone. Offering or agreeing to help others is not about submerging all your own needs and priorities. Help if and when you can. Say *"No"* when you can't or don't want to. Do it firmly and politely. If appropriate, re-direct them towards people who can and would be prepared to help them. Some of the time, you won't be able to help directly. But it's highly likely, other members of your network will be able to offer valuable help.

People who can say "No" and refuse to be taken for a ride find that they are thought MORE of, not less.

A friend and fellow professional speaker once said to me *"I don't mind recommending good speakers, but I'd never recommend someone better than me."* I said *"Funnily enough, I would want to do the opposite because I'd know the speaker would go down really well. That would reflect positively on the organiser, who would think more of me. Whereas, if the speaker wasn't as good, my reputation would suffer. It also forces me to make more of an effort when I'M speaking!"*

Top performers are team players. They share. They look out for opportunities for those they know. They actively seek alliances. They encourage collaboration. Sales, information, support and other opportunities, appear as if from nowhere when you are prepared to give and receive help.

They benefit from the leverage it gives them from a virtual team of supporters - people who volunteer to hand out a stream of profitable opportunities.

Questions to ask yourself

▮▶ What do people say about you behind your back?

▮▶ Are you perceived as a 'giver' or a 'taker'?

▮▶ What about your company?

▮▶ How many referrals do you give?

▮▶ What about your company? How many referrals do your colleagues offer to customers, or those who are simply not in a position to be a customer yet?

> "*When you are wrapped up in yourself, you make for a very small parcel*". Anonymous

In Ivan Misner PhD and Robert Davis' book *Business By Referral*, they introduce the GAINS Exchange - the five things you and all your contacts should know about each other, to create a more meaningful relationship to start a two way flow of referrals;

G Their personal, business, financial and educational GOALS.

A ACCOMPLISHMENTS. What you are each most proud of. These give an invaluable insight into your values and beliefs.

I INTERESTS. What you most enjoy doing, discussing, collecting, watching or listening to.

N NETWORKS The personal, professional, religious, sporting and community networks you belong to that include members who could be potential customers for each other.

S SKILLS. The specific skills you each possess and at what level of proficiency.

Be proactive, yet relaxed and low key about finding out this stuff from those you know and meet. Share your own information too.

Actively seeking opportunities to give referrals will prepare the ground for you to receive more. They probably won't necessarily come back from the same people. That's OK. Have faith. It works. And it's why we are looking at offering referrals first.

My credo has always been "*I devote my life to being someone who is worth knowing. It has served me well. I believe deeply that this is at the heart of true success in business.*"

Offering Help and Referrals

Who are the people you know well who consistently demonstrate an abundance mentality? Help them first. Tell them that you have noticed they are always helping others - ask how you can be of assistance to them. Here you will probably face your first problem; most people don't actually know what they want.

As part of an exercise at my seminars I deliberately ask delegates to sit down quietly and make a list of the help they would appreciate. The majority find it extremely difficult at first. So don't be surprised if your initial offer is batted back with a *"No, I'm fine."* Politely and sincerely make eye contact and say *"I'm serious. I would like to see if I can help you in any way. I may be able to find new business for you. But I can't do that unless I'm absolutely clear about what you want."* Some people (especially those with a scarcity mindset) avoid asking for help because it can make them feel uncomfortable, afraid they will 'owe' a return favour. Be sincere and say *"This is an offer, I don't expect anything in return."* Obviously, don't bother to make such offers to people you know who are seriously and serially self-focused!

Encourage those you want to help to think further about what they need. Follow up on your offers. Remain low key and polite. Respect any hesitance. Build trust. Gently encourage them to speak more openly about their needs. Asking personal questions is a sensitive issue. It is not always appropriate. Anyone who perceives you as 'pumping them for information' will distrust you.

Requests could include just about anything; where they can buy particular products or services, locating a new supplier, specific business information, advice on any number of domestic issues, or a request to be a 'sounding board'.

▮▶ Do you have expertise on useful subjects/topics, your contacts may not know about? Make a point of educating your contacts about what you can offer them.

⏩ What are you most knowledgeable about?

⏩ Write to all of your friends, colleagues, and customers asking for information, in order to be on the lookout for them

⏩ Study your clients' websites, brochures and other marketing materials, to get a better sense of what they are about.

⏩ Part of your role is to become an extra pair of eyes and ears for your contacts.

⏩ Encourage your contacts to talk about their achievements, what they are most proud of and their business aspirations. Try to figure out ways you can help them achieve their ambitions.

⏩ You can then ask them about their problems.

⏩ Be a partner with clients who are open to it and with everyone you do business with.

⏩ Offer to be their unofficial head of promotion. Part of your duties would include making a point of speaking well of them behind their back, when you meet prospective new clients for them. Feed back the names of those you meet in this way and what you said. It's fantastic to be able to re-connect with your contacts by telling them what wonderful things you have been saying about them.

⏩ When you receive a request for help, what is your contact expecting from you personally? What is your own time commitment? What do you intend to do? By when? What are you NOT agreeing to? Be very clear on all these issues. Manage expectations and establish parameters. If something involves too much time, say so at the outset. Remember, this is not a voluntary slave labour programme. So, don't over-commit yourself.

⏸ You need to know exactly what they are looking for. Your help has to be of value to them. Sending unsuitable opportunities or inappropriate information is a waste of everyone's time - yours included.

⏸ If they are say, looking for products, are they interested in new or second-hand? In what price range? Where have they looked already? What other preferences do they have? Why?

⏸ Is the request an immediate need, or are they merely toying with the idea? What specific skills is the person looking for? What type of supplier would be most or least suitable? Who have they tried already? Asking these questions demonstrates how serious you are about offering the best help or referral. By qualifying the request, you will also minimise the possibility of building up the hopes of your supplier contact only to have them dashed, when told they didn't intend to do anything after all.

⏸ In many industries, competition is more intense than ever before. But few people like to volunteer the fact that business isn't as brisk as they would like it to be. Until you establish trust, they may be a bit guarded or try to put on a brave face. Avoid asking *"How's business?"* Instead, focus on finding out what new business they want. What are their business objectives and priorities? Sometimes the mere fact you ask these types of questions helps them think more clearly about their business.

⏸ Don't assume you know what they want. Let them tell you themselves.

❿ Really listen. Look at the person when they are speaking to you. Give your undivided attention.

❿ Make a point of asking this question after you've shared your expertise *"How useful has this been?"* It provides valuable feedback on your worth and helps them to realise how helpful you are being. When they say it aloud, they are more likely to remember your usefulness.

❿ If there's a business opportunity for someone else, don't provide the same offer to more than one person, under the mistaken belief that all of them will be receiving a referral. I've heard of people who give one opportunity to eight competing companies. This is no longer a referral. Just a 'lead'. Unless there's a specific reason for putting forward a few choices, they'll all get annoyed with you for wasting their time.

❿ If you can't help personally, say so and add *"I will ask around for you. I'll get back to you in x hours or days to tell you what I've managed to find out."* Make sure you do, or explain promptly the reason for any delay.

❿ Important; Build a reputation for sticking to your word. Nothing will undermine your credibility and reputation faster than breaking your promises. You would have been better off not offering help in the first place.

❿ Ask yourself who has the necessary skills, knowledge or contacts to find a solution to your contact's problems. Call or email those most likely to have the answers. Tell them the request is on behalf of your friend or customer. This achieves a number of things;

- by tapping into a wider pool of knowledge, you increase the likelihood you will solve the problem,

- it's a great way to re-connect with others in your network
- it demonstrates to those you contact that you are looking after the interests of others and
- you may be calling to offer them some business.

▶ Follow up on the referrals you give. Keep everyone in the loop. Call each party and ask how things are progressing.

▶ Offer a free consultation or other help to the friends and colleagues of your existing customers. Make it 'No risk. No obligation.' It's a service to your customer and someone they think might benefit from meeting you. Position it as a favour rather than a referral request. If they trust you, they will probably want to do this for their friend.

▶ Draw up a list of the people who you trust the most and who trust you. Sit down with them to brainstorm opportunities for each other.

A Few Words of Warning

Sometimes your generosity may be abused. This will happen sooner or later. Realise this now. And accept it.

For example, I no longer mention prospective clients or customers in front of one particular associate because in the past, he has called those clients and claimed to have been given the referral, when in fact he hadn't! Trust was broken. End of relationship.

▶ Some people simply don't want a relationship with you. They will shun your offers of help. Accept this. It's probably nothing to do with you. They could be clinically distrustful of the motives of everyone they meet. Unless you want to be an unpaid counsellor or therapist, leave them alone. Focus your energies on those most likely to appreciate your support.

Be a Mentor or Coach

The best mentors and coaches do not get physically involved in tasks - their function is to guide, question and support when needed. As a mentor, you can learn from the mentee's behaviour, ways of working and where they find information.

Find a mentor for yourself too. Who you get advice from is one of the keys to your future success. Choose one who 'walks their talk'. Ask individuals to recommend others who may be prepared to help you. You do not need to limit yourself to one person. There is little point in listening to those people who have never made it themselves. Indeed, listening to the wrong people will hold you back.

Build Trust and Rapport

Knowing how to build rapport with everyone you meet, whether male or female, is one of the most valuable communication skills you can acquire. Rapport building skills will greatly influence your success at generating referrals.

I'm sure you can think of people who have an amazing ability to make others feel comfortable, appreciated, important and understood, even within moments of meeting them for the first time. For many it's totally intuitive, they don't know how they do it. Some rapport experts can meet someone new, and get to total intimacy in less than 10 minutes! The great news is, if your rapport building is not as good as you'd like it to be, it can be learned. And you can get really good at it if you want to. But I can't guarantee you'll get intimate with everyone you meet in less than 10 minutes!!

Your first task when meeting someone new is for them to get a sense of knowing, liking, trusting and valuing you. No relationship can develop at any level until rapport has been built. We've already discussed a crucial element of rapport building - namely asking questions which encourage those you meet to open up to you. This approach will help you find common ground.

So what do you have in common? I'm sure you have met people who were quite cool towards you, until you made a small comment about where you were brought up, what school or college you went to, or even where you went on holiday when you were a kid. They latch on to your experiences and memories,

because they share them. By asking appropriate questions about the experiences of people, it is usually possible to find some areas of common interest - do you have children, a cat or dog. A word of warning; Don't claim you have something in common if you don't, under the mistaken idea that it will help you to build rapport. You'll only succeed in demonstrating that you are a fraud - who obviously has a hidden agenda and you will not be trusted. Building rapport effectively is all about creating trust, and it requires honesty and integrity.

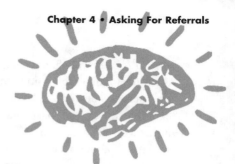

Chapter 4

Your PeoplePortfolio® Referral Plan

Part 2 - Asking for Help and Referrals

Implementing a formal referral generating system has the power to double, or even triple your business, by bringing in more new customers than you might think possible. Just imagine for a moment how much new business you could attract if you had more than one system for referrals.

Gaining new clients, customers or patients needn't be a problem for you and your business ever again. There are ways you can ask for lots of referrals and feel good about it - but you do have to ask for them! If you can't or won't ask for referrals - get therapy or read on. But first...

What's Stopping You From Receiving More Referrals

⏵ Is your business worthy of being referred? Do your customers like you and value what you offer? If not, you need to make improvements BEFORE you implement any referral programme. Fully research what is not working within your business. Ask your customers, suppliers, colleagues in which ways your competitors are out-performing you - on price, level of service, delivery, product reliability, innovation, depth of knowledge, quality of advice. Get all this stuff right.

▮ Asking for referrals fills so many people with dread, it makes them feel vulnerable, uncomfortable or even sick in the stomach. So guess what? They won't do it! Bad or unsuccessful experiences in the past may colour your thoughts and influence your behaviour. If you've failed to generate referrals or felt bad about asking for them, it's not surprising that you won't be that enthusiastic about doing it again. This is fully understandable. However, these beliefs could be costing you loads of business. Until you feel confident and comfortable about asking for referrals - you won't. Simple as that. Turning a negative experience into a positive one is all that stands between you and referral success.

▮ Some will interpret your desire for referrals as a sign that your business is not going too well. This type of 'skewed' thinking must be addressed by helping them to realise that it's only the best and most successful businesses that receive referrals.

▮ Others are 'too busy' and don't want to get involved.

▮ Offering help to people we know, like, trust and value makes us feel really good about ourselves. Why should your customers feel any differently about helping you, when they know that you go out of your way to look after their best interests?

The truth is; many of your customers would LOVE to give you referrals. If only they knew you wanted their help. Perhaps you put enormous energy into conveying a professional image to your customers. To them, you might appear so successful it wouldn't even cross their minds that you are looking for more business. This carefully crafted image and perception you have created could be costing you a huge amount in lost business.

What Help and Support to Ask For

▶ Ask more people for their advice. It's often quite flattering for them and can save you time and money. Why try to re-invent the wheel, when there are people you know who already have the experience you seek?

▶ If it makes you feel better, at first limit your help requests to those that require very little time or effort on the part of the 'giver'.

▶ What help and advice could you benefit from right now? Make a list of everything.

▶ Go through all your outstanding tasks.

▶ Ask yourself who could help with ideas, resources, insight, solutions and contacts, relating to business as well as personal and domestic matters.

▶ Perhaps you'd like some help learning how to use a particular piece of computer software?

▶ Or you are looking to buy a new electrical appliance? Which companies offer the best prices and guarantees?

▶ Would you benefit from hiring a freelancer on a part time or project basis? Who could find one for you?

▶ Who do you know who has the answers to these queries and would be prepared to share them with you?

▶ Carry your 'Help List' around with you. Refer to it often. And keep it up to date.

❱❱ This list can prove very useful. After you have helped someone else, or you have delivered an outstanding service to a customer, they are likely to say *"If there's anything I can ever do for you, please feel free to ask."* Our usual response is to smile and say *"If I ever think of anything, I'll let you know."* Of course, you never will. Either you won't think of anything they can do for you or, if you do, you talk yourself out of following up their offer. You'll tell yourself that they were only being polite. Or what if I ask them and they've forgotten about the offer? It would be embarrassing for them as well as for me. The result - you lose out.

It's so much better when anyone makes such an offer to say. *"Thank you. Your offer is really appreciated. In the past when customers offered their help in this way, I could never think of anything at the time, so I have got into the habit of writing down the help I would most appreciate as it occurs to me."*

Take out your Help List, scan it and mention the most appropriate items. Invariably, if your customer knows you fairly well, they will ask to see what else is on the list. Show it. This will almost certainly lead to a more detailed conversation and generate far more ways they can help you. You might like to offer it in the style of a waiter handing over a restaurant menu. Depending on their sense of humour - take their order! Include on your list a succinct description of your ideal customer profile, and the telltale signs of how a contact would spot a potential customer for you.

❱❱ Tell them how invaluable your Help List has been to you. Suggest they develop their own and share it with those they know, like, trust and value. Ask to see it when they've finished, to see if there's any way you can help them too.

❱❱ Be sensitive about how much time and effort your request for help may require.

▮ Offer to do a skills or knowledge swap with key contacts.

▮ Keep a list of the help you have been asked for by your contacts.

▮ When looking for advice, make a point of asking more than one person. You will get a more balanced view.

▮ Only ask people who have a high degree of knowledge and skill about that specific issue. For example, if you want financial advice, are they qualified to give it? Avoid those who are quick to offer opinions that can't be backed up with expertise.

▮ Ensure the person does not feel under any pressure to comply with your request. Give them the opportunity to say "*No*". They may be particularly busy at that precise moment. If they are unable to help, ask for any suggestions of others you could ask.

▮ Don't ask consultants for their advice unless you are prepared to pay for it. They sell advice for a living. If you know a consultant well, they may not mind giving you some of their time for free, but don't expect or assume they will.

▮ Strategically identify key people you want to do business with. Prospective clients who hear from a number of sources at the same time, suggesting that you are the person or company to solve their problems, can be particularly convincing. When you have targeted a specific potential client, find a number of people who know this individual and are prepared to speak well of you. Ask each one to contact the prospect on your behalf. When you eventually make contact, they will have already heard of you and are satisfied that you are worth talking to.

Who to Ask

"Everybody" would be the reflex answer. Don't.... instead, focus your limited time asking those who already know, like, trust and value you. These people are the most likely to provide you with high quality referrals. Success with these individuals will help you feel more comfortable when asking for referrals in the future. As your experience increases you will be more likely to want to cast your net wider.

▮▶ First of all, target everyone you know who is most likely to want to help you. Dismiss no-one.

> *I learned this lesson the hard way. By 1981 I had spent two years sending out hundreds of letters to radio and TV companies, asking for an opportunity to work as a broadcaster. I got nowhere. Utterly depressed about my lack of success, I went home to my parents. My mother wanted to know why I was so 'down'. Once I explained, she said "You need to speak to my cousin. He's a director at the BBC!" "Why on earth didn't you tell me?" said I. Her response was "You never asked!" She set it all up. Her cousin Phil introduced me to a senior BBC producer, that led to an audition. Ten days later I started presenting my own radio programme! My mistake was to assume that those closest to me would not be able to help. Include immediate and extended family, long term friends, past colleagues and, most importantly, your closest customers and clients - the people you would choose to have as friends. Ask every one of these people for their help and support.*

▮▶ Don't make the mistake that some people you know lack influence or power. All too often they are the ones who know many successful individuals who place a great deal of trust in their opinions. They are relied on for down-to-earth, honest feedback. The fact that you are seen to look after the 'little' people reinforces the notion that you are someone who can be trusted to look after them too.

⚫ Re-connect with existing and past clients.

⚫ Instigate a system for educating your newest clients to think about providing you with referrals. Then ask them.

⚫ Non-customers can be added to your target lists further down the line.

Before You Ask

⚫ First, who do you most want as clients, customers or patients? Clearly describe in writing your ideal customer profile. If you have more than one profile, define each one in as much detail as possible. Which customers are the most profitable? Who are the least demanding of your time or energy? Who are the most valuable for additional referral business?

⚫ Define potential customers by age, gender, ethnicity, income level, geographic location, the size of company, an individual's position within the company, their buying power or responsibility, membership of common interest groups, trade associations, business organisations.

⚫ Next, who DON'T you want as clients, customers or patients? Why?

It's only by going through this exercise will you be able to help your referral sources to become focused enough to help you.

When to Ask

More and more companies, especially one-person businesses, are coming to realise they have a finite amount of time to devote to each customer. Traditional customer acquisition costs can be high. It also takes a lot of time, time that could be better invested satisfying and developing business with their existing customers. This is why some companies are becoming increasingly selective about who they take on as a new client. One of the ways they assess the eligibility of a prospective client is, by making it a condition at the outset of doing business, that they will provide the company with high quality referrals in the future, once they are satisfied with product and service delivery. If a client is not prepared to do this, they are simply not taken on. In these cases, referrals are on the agenda even before anyone is allowed to become a customer or client.

Assuming your service quality is high, prospective customers are usually not put off by this approach. Invariably they may respond positively and think more of you, not less. This is especially true if they have been introduced to you through a referral. It says *"They must be good if they have the confidence to do this."*

▶ Tell every new customer at the earliest possible moment in your relationship, that your entire business or service is based on satisfying your customers, clients or patients so much they choose to recommend their friends, family and colleagues. Howard Shenson wrote about *"Planting referral seeds of suggestion, allowing them to mature and bear fruit."* Make this an integral part of the way you interact with all customers. This prepares the ground for a time when you will ask each of them for referrals.

▶ When a client offers a compliment about what you have done for them, ask for a referral at that time. Don't delay your request. They are at their most receptive to the idea of offering referrals. Say *"We are always looking for new clients. We'd like to be able to help your friends and colleagues too. Seeing as you are so happy with what we are doing, who do you know who we should be talking to?"* If they say they can't think of anyone, reply *"I wouldn't expect you to be able think of anyone now. When can we discuss this properly?"*

▶ Learn to identify the moments when customers are most happy with your products or services. You have just delivered the product or service on time, or on budget. You've given them some invaluable help or advice beyond what they could reasonably expect. These are good times to ask - if you do it in the right way.

▶ Asking for referrals 'out of the blue' is never recommended. No-one likes to be put on the spot. Instead, help your contacts get used to the idea of giving you referrals, before you actually ask for them. To do this, start to mention to your contacts how many referrals you seem to be receiving since it became a focus of your business. For some, they won't know that you are looking for more business. Others won't care! Then add *"Maybe be one day we could explore who you know who might also want to work with us?"* Make a mental note about how each person responds to these 'off the cuff' remarks? Obviously, those who show a high degree of interest in helping you, should be given the opportunity to do so! But for the rest, say *"I would like to discuss it further at some time. How would you feel about that?"* Notice how they respond to that question too. Then carry on with what you were doing or talking about.

▶ Give your contact the opportunity to discuss referrals there and then, or make an appointment. Sometimes it's better to set up a specific meeting. You appear more professional and less 'desperate'. And it takes the pressure off, by giving them more time to think about potential people for you.

When NOT to Ask

Until people know, like, trust and value you, referrals are less likely. If anyone thinks you are using them, they won't want to help you. Insincerity kills your chances of referrals.

▮▶ All relationships go through high and low points. Asking for referrals at a low point is not a good idea. Check that nothing is happening between your organisation and your contact, which might hinder your attempts to generate referrals. Call the person to ask if everything is going well. If there are problems, don't ask for referrals. Offer to correct the problem instead. Once you have done so, meet up to discuss how the problem has been remedied. If you sense the customer is particularly pleased with the outcome - that's the time to ask for referrals.

▮▶ If the person feels under any emotional pressure to comply with your request, you will meet resistance, hesitance or a flat refusal.

▮▶ If someone says *"No"*. Find out why. There could be a whole load of different reasons why they have refused. Don't let it go. However, grabbing them by the throat as part of your approach is not advised! Do it in a low key, polite way. Perhaps start by saying *"I respect your decision. Lots of people choose to recommend us. Is there any particular reason you don't feel able to do so at this time?"* Including *"at this time"* creates room for a change of mind in the future. Go on to explain *"We don't want anyone to do this unless they are delighted to do so. What would I need to do so that you would want to recommend us in the future?"* Listen carefully to what is said. DO NOT try to change their mind, defend yourself or argue your case.

▮ Ask *"Is it a good time to talk?"* If your potential referral source is under stress, time pressure or is pre-occupied in any way, don't ask, you won't receive the attention you need. Nor should you ask if you are under similar pressures - your request may appear more desperate or 'hungry' than you are! This is hardly surprising when so many salespeople believe they are set such 'outrageous' sales targets to hit each month!

▮ Thanking a customer for their support by giving them a gift is NOT the time to ask for a referral. It could be interpreted as a bribe.

> *A highly successful Multi-Level Marketing salesperson once told me a delicious story of an American, who visited Britain to 'teach' his referral technique. He brushed aside anything he was told about how the British and European culture was different to North America. He said "Take me to a rail station at peak time, and I'll show you how to get referrals." He went into his 'patter'. Not only was he unsuccessful - two people hit him!*

How to Ask

Throwing away your request will probably throw away any opportunity. Position your request for help as something that's important to you. When you have decided the time has arrived to ask specific people for referrals try the following approach. Most people don't mind giving 'advice'. Say to your contact *"I'd really appreciate your advice. Would you help me please?"* They are less likely to be put off if you start your conversation in this way. Go on to say *"I'm looking to grow my business and would appreciate any advice you might have about who else you think I should contact. Who do you know who...?* This 'soft' approach is based on Mark Sheer's technique but allows you to back off if the person isn't willing or able to help you at that time. Ask these people when it would be a good time to have a conversation.

Your objective is clear - you want names. Therefore, your first task is to unlock those names from your source's brain, without appearing too pushy, keen or desperate. Bill Cates asks for permission to 'Brainstorm'. This is an inspired way to position your referral discussion.

At the outset, your contacts may be unsure about whether they can help you. They are perhaps a little anxious about the possibility of letting you down. Most people find it difficult to think of the names of people you should speak to. They are not being difficult, usually they know so many people they could choose from, they don't know where to start. Inevitably, they suffer from temporary mental paralysis. This may make them feel bad or inadequate. It's your job to help them feel relaxed and under no pressure.

Potential referral sources will feel more at ease if they are only being asked to 'brainstorm'. Explain that it's quite common for people's minds to go blank at the beginning of your conversation. Add that those who have agreed to provide referrals also tend to eliminate some people, because they are not sure if they would be interested. Ask them not to de-select names. In reality, for some reason, those individuals always seem to turn out to be the best referrals!

Important; DO NOT say *"Do you know anyone who...?"* If no-one comes to mind at that precise moment, they'll say *"No, I can't think of anyone."* They effectively press the delete key in their brain. Subject closed.

A better question is *"Who do you know who...?"* This forces the brain to seek out appropriate people. If the person can't think of anyone instantly, their brain is likely to keep searching until it comes up with someone. Don't be surprised if they contact you a *few hours or days later to say "I've just thought of someone."*

These questions will help them to focus on specific people you could meet;

‣ What business organisations do they belong to with members who would most likely benefit from your products/services? Instead of 'business organisations' substitute 'special interest', 'hobby', 'religious', 'sport' and 'social' organisations.

‣ Who are the people they choose to spend most time with at their events? Why them?

‣ Which colleagues and former colleagues do you choose to be with?

▶ Do not interrupt their thought processes. Do not ask them for the contacts details or additional information about anyone they mention. Simply listen and write down their names calmly and quietly. Curb your initial excitement at the prospect of meeting all these potentially profitable customers! Only when they have finished giving names should you go back to ask for the contact details of each person, and any additional or relevant information they can share about them.

Before You Contact The Referral

Learn as much as you can about the referral from the source. Position this research as something that helps ensure you tailor a solution to the particular needs of the referral. Use this information to help them look good by recommending you. Ask some, not all of these questions:

- How do they know the referral?
- Why does the source think they are a likely customer or client for you?
- Who is their existing supplier, if any?
- What specific products or services do they think the referral will be most interested in? Why?
- Do they have a specific need for what you offer, or are they only looking at their options?
- What specific problems, anxieties or business pressures are they having to deal with?
- How sensitive would they be about you knowing this?
- Do they have the power to make a buying decision or will they need to pass it on to their superiors for approval?
- What other background information would help you serve them better?

❚❯ Sometimes the source won't want to give you the details of the referral, and will suggest they speak to the person on your behalf. They will call you if they are interested. If or when the referral calls you, position yourself as a helpful person. Say *"As a friend (or colleague) of [name of source], I would be delighted to help you in any way I can. What can I do for you?"*

❚❯ Think about the factors that could stop people referring business to you. What if it doesn't turn out well? How badly could it reflect on the person who offered the referral? And what can you do to alleviate or even eliminate any fear and anxiety these people may have? What sort of guarantees can you offer?

❚❯ Rather than leave it entirely up to the referral to call you, say *"I realise that you might be feeling nervous about giving me their details in case they are not interested, so why don't you call or email them to ask if they would appreciate a call from me?"* This demonstrates you understand and respect their sensitivity. Some may then decide to give you the contact details any way.

How to Contact the Referral

Ideally, your source will contact the referral on your behalf before you call or write. Ask if they would be prepared to do this for you. Explain that, by doing so, you won't be a stranger to them when you make contact personally.

Focus on how helpful this support will be to the person being referred. In order to help them even more, gently ask your source to tell the referral a little about you,

- What you have done for them,
- How reasonable your prices were,
- How professional and reliable you are and
- Why they think you should both meet. Any relevant information could be included.

⏵ Ask the source to tell the referral that you are prepared to offer a free no obligation conversation/consultation. By speaking well of you 'behind your back', they will help you significantly shorten the time it takes to build the necessary trust and credibility to convert a referral into a customer.

⏵ Find out when they will be able to make contact with the referral. Say that you will not contact the referral until they have. If possible, agree a time when you will re-connect with the source to confirm that the referral is expecting to hear from you. Use this call as an opportunity to learn about what was said during their conversation. You may discover the referral has an immediate need, or perhaps they are only researching their options. This information will help you prepare for your initial contact. Promise to keep the source informed about what happens - either way. Keep your word on this. Sometimes the referral won't want you to contact them. This is OK. How come? It saves embarrassment for the source and the referral - and saves your precious time.

⏵ Your biggest fans will offer or agree to be present at your first meeting. Invite the source to join you for the lunch or social drink. You pick up the entire tab.

⏵ Not everyone will feel they have the time to do all of this for you. That's OK too. WARNING Realise whatever someone offers or is prepared to do for you is OK. Your sources always control the relationship with their contacts. YOU DO NOT HAVE CONTROL. If you try to take control away from your source in any way, you run a very high risk of ruining the referral. Even more importantly, you could sour the relationship so much, the source won't volunteer referrals to you in the future. I have seen too many over-zealous salespeople trying to 'help' the process by speeding it up too soon. Work with what you are given.

‣ Equipped with detailed background information on your referral, agree with your source the best way to make your initial contact. Once again, position yourself as someone who is offering to help.

‣ Important; make contact immediately when you have agreed your approach with the source. You do not want the source to ask a couple of days/weeks later if you have contacted the referral for you to reply *"I haven't got around to it yet."* This says that you have other higher priorities, meaning that their help is not that important!

‣ If telephoning, say *"Hello. [Name of source] has asked me to promise to contact you, because he/she believes I may be able to offer you some help or advice. My name is [your name]. How can I help you?"* Then pause. Chances are, the referral won't know at this stage what help you can assist them with. Perhaps they haven't spoken to your source about you. If you sense this, go on to say *"[Name of source] told me you were researching your options about [product or service they are looking for] and thought I might be able to give you some useful advice about it."*

Note: give your source's name first. This will be more likely to put them at ease than if you gave your name first. By calling/writing because you promised your source to do it is another way of helping to convince the referral that you are making contact for their benefit not yours. Offering advice reinforces your role as someone they would want to talk to.

‣ If you sense it isn't a good time to talk, bring up the subject before the referral does. Ask when it would be convenient for you to meet? Arrange to meet or schedule another call.

‣ A letter or email constructed along the same lines will be most likely to generate a follow up meeting or conversation. With an email, send a 'cc' copy to your source. The referral will see that you have done this, and feel reassured that you are really contacting them because of your source.

After Your Initial Contact

▮▶ IMPORTANT Find the time to thank everyone who offers help to you. Do so in writing. Preferably use a fountain pen. Send a hand written card or a letter. Emails are OK, but not as effective. Develop this habit as a priority. Sending 'thank you' notes is taught on the most basic sales training courses. Even so, only a tiny proportion of people actually do it. To convince yourself of its significance, think of a time when you have gone out of your way for someone, and received nothing to say that it was helpful, no thanks, and no news about how things worked out or not. What did that feel like?

Don't believe there's no time for it. It only takes a few seconds, costs just a few pence and will set you apart from most of the population. In your note, tell the person how much you appreciated their advice, support, insight or the trust they placed in you, by giving you the name and number of one of their contacts. Reassure them that you will respect their relationship with the contact.

▮▶ An essential element of referrals is to keep in touch with your source. Remember to follow up with both a personal note and a call. Re-connecting with your referral sources is absolutely crucial if you are to be successful at generating even more referrals in the future.

▮▶ Contact them again whether you have something to report or not. Few people thank sources for those that don't work out. So long as the referral fitted your customer profile, show appreciation for their desire to help you. It's so important to keep all your supporters 'in the loop'.

▮▶ If appropriate, send them a small gift to express your appreciation. Gifts are a way of saying thank you - they are not, nor should they be construed as a payment or commission. Indeed, some companies and government bodies may restrict or forbid the receiving of gifts.

▮▶ You won't be successful every time you contact a referral. However, referrals who can't or won't do business with you are prime candidates to refer you to their own contacts, because you have been highly recommended by someone they probably know, like, trust and value. Remember to include comments about why so many of your customers choose to recommend your services. This starts the process of generating even more referrals from your referrals.

After the Sale

▮▶ Always thank your customer for the business. Do so sincerely and tell the customer that you are absolutely committed to help them in any way you can in the future.

▮▶ Scott Kramnick suggests asking *"Is there anything you would like me to improve to make it more likely you would be prepared to recommend my services to the people you know and like?"* And

▮▶ *"I'm curious. Who have you mentioned me to? What did you say?"*

▮▶ Tell them you would like to keep in touch. Perhaps you can write to them in 6 months or a year, by sending your quarterly newsletter. Make sure they do not think you plan to pester them in the future.

▶ Ask if it is acceptable for you to re-connect with them.

▶ Schedule a follow up in your diary or contact management database for three, six or twelve months' time.

▶ Reassure the customer that they made a wise buying decision.

▶ Educate the customer to make the best use of their purchase and tell them how to maintain it in top condition.

▶ Stress that you are available to them at any time in the future, if they have any questions or requests. Give them your contact details, if they do not have them.

By doing the above, you will be preparing the ground for future referral opportunities. Once a customer has had a positive experience of your product or service over a longer period, they will be even more likely to offer referrals. They have a lot of confidence in the product or service quality. And they have seen on-going evidence of your commitment to after-sales service. They probably didn't expect it, which makes it even more impressive. However, the majority of sales people are too busy chasing new prospects to fully harness these huge referral opportunities.

Chapter 5

Your PeoplePortfolio® Referral Plan

Part 3 - Testimonial Power

What customers and clients are prepared to say about you in writing can be immensely valuable as referrals. In this chapter we will look at how to apply a simple process to increase the number, quality and type of testimonials you will receive, and then make maximum use of them to increase your sales.

Testimonials from high-calibre executives have probably contributed more to the success of my own business over the past 20 years, than any other marketing initiative. When a Chief Executive of a large European merchant bank saw that I had a testimonial from a highly respected CEO of another company, he said *"If John feels this way about this guy, he should work with us"*.

Testimonials are a form of referral no-one should ignore. They are INCREDIBLY powerful when used appropriately. Most companies, even those that use testimonials, don't even scratch the surface of their full potential. How many letters do you and your company have right now from satisfied or delighted customers? If they are sitting in a filing cabinet gathering dust, or framed in your reception area, you are wasting a valuable resource.

Why Bother with Testimonials?

People need reassuring they will not be making a mistake when doing business with you. High quality testimonials provide that reassurance. No matter how much you or your company spends on advertising, PR and promotion, prospective customers will attach more credibility and attention to third parties, who have used your products and services for themselves. A 'paid for' endorsement, perhaps by a celebrity, is not the same as a customer testimonial. Real customers, who have NOT been paid to make their comments, carry more weight.

Obviously, the quality of your products, levels of service and the results you help to create for your customers and clients, must be high for this stuff to work!

I urge you to start collecting and using testimonials. It is so much more effective to tell people how wonderful you are through the words of others - especially if they are highly respected in their industry. You will benefit from their professional reputations and integrity. When I recommend to people that they start collecting them - I often get the initial response, *"But I don't know anyone who I could ask."* They tend to be the people who end up with the best ones.

Step 1 - What to do First

Look for the testimonials you already have. Go through your files to find every customer letter you have received which includes positive comments. Don't worry at this stage about who they are from, when they were written or if the remark seems insignificant.

▶ Make two photocopies of each document.

▶ Use one copy to highlight the words, phrases and paragraphs with the best comments.

▶ Type up all of these comments into one document, including the name of the individual and the organisation they are from.

▮ Send the second copy, with a note explaining that you are *"planning to use a collection of testimonials from past customers who have written to say how pleased they were with 'our products/services. We would be extremely keen to use an extract from the enclosed letter you wrote to us. Please could we have permission to use what you wrote?"* Highlight the relevant text. If the letter is quite old and they are still an active customer, perhaps they could be persuaded to update the letter for you, by including additional comments. Ask them. Anyone who goes to the trouble to write and tell you how pleased they are, is more likely to agree to such a request.

▮ Study the testimonials you already have. What do you notice? Are there common threads running through them? Do they tend to focus on one or two elements of your service? Perhaps there aren't many testimonials in your files. This could mean a number of different things. Is it a sign that you need to improve your business? If this isn't the case - may be your customers tell you in person how pleased they are.

Step 2 - Identify Your Fans

Who are your 'best' customers and clients? What about your best suppliers? It's worth defining 'best'. These are not necessarily the people who do the most business with you. They are those who speak well of you 'behind your back', are well known, well respected and/or influential within their industry. If they also spend a lot with you - so much the better!

If you don't know the names of your customers because your company uses distributors or wholesalers, try to find out. Selling direct to customers is a major concern amongst intermediaries. Many keep suppliers away from their customers, afraid that they will be bypassed. So long as you don't plan to do this, reassure your distribution channel that this is not the case - indeed, the testimonials you are looking for will help them sell more.

⏵ List all of your best customers and clients.

⏵ Starting with those you have the best relationship with, speak to each of them (preferably face-to-face). Say you would appreciate their help and advice. Tell them you are looking to grow your business. Briefly explain that you want to compile a series of testimonials from your most valued customers. *"I obviously thought of you."* Then say *"If you think our (products/service/work) deserves a testimonial I would be delighted to receive one from you."* Add *"How would you feel about providing my company with a testimonial?"*

⏵ If they agree, follow the conversation up with a short personalised letter. Do it quickly - within a day or so. The longer you delay the follow up, the less likely you'll receive the testimonial. More than a week and the response will drop off substantially.

In my experience, if someone agrees to do something for you verbally, they can easily forget. This can make it difficult to follow up - a reminder sometimes offends, because its effectively telling them that they are inefficient and unreliable! Don't be tempted to follow up with an email instead of a letter. email culture gives people permission NOT to respond. So stick with a letter, which is more tangible. Most people eventually reply to their mail.

The wording in your letter is important. Thank them for agreeing to provide you with a testimonial. Tell them how much you are looking forward to receiving it. Then include *"I/we have found that testimonials from highly respected individuals goes a long way towards allaying any fears or anxieties new clients may have about doing business with a new supplier."* I've found this sentence to be particularly effective at generating a positive letter. The 'highly respected individuals' phrase embedded within the sentence appeals to the recipient's ego.

I▶ Include a first class stamped self-addressed envelope for the reply.

I▶ Occasionally, delighted customers will agree, but hesitate because they don't know what to write. Help them to help you by suggesting their letter focus on a particular aspect of your business relationship that they appreciate more than any other.

I▶ Ask them to comment on specific aspects of your company's claims of uniqueness or expertise. They will find it easier to write when given such guidance. See later in this chapter for more on this issue.

I▶ Other customers may be busy and ask you to write it for them. Personally, I don't like to do this, simply because you will hold back too much. You won't want them to think that you've used too many adjectives - so the testimonial won't be as good. For these people, offer to interview them instead. Write down their responses. Condense what they actually said into the testimonial. Send it by email, invite them to make any alterations and print it on their company letterhead. Most of the time they won't make any changes.

Interview questions could include the following;

I▶ How long have they been a customer?

I▶ What do they value most highly about your work, product or service?

I▶ How happy are they to be a customer?

▶ What results do your products or service help them to deliver?

▶ How is their business/life improved as a result of using your products?

▶ How easy is it to do business with you?

▶ Why do they continue to do business with you?

▶ Do they plan to remain a customer? If so, why?

▶ Are there any people from within your organisation who deserve to be mentioned? Why? (Circulating letters internally which mention members of staff by name is a great staff motivational tool).

▶ How well are you looked after as a customer?

▶ What would you say about us to someone who has never heard of us? (This last question normally generates a fascinating insight that you will want to use within the testimonial.)

Step 3 - Build a System and Testimonials Will Come

After you've identified, contacted and generated testimonials from your known fans, you need a system to generate future testimonials from the rest of your customers.

▶ Identify key customers with the highest profile or influence within your different markets. Focus energy on gaining testimonials from these people.

▶ Create a template letter, thanking the customer for their

business and requesting a testimonial, based on the letter mentioned earlier.

⑩ Decide on an appropriate time to send your letter. How long will they need to fully appreciate what they have bought from you? For example, for my work as a conference moderator and speaker, I send out a letter within a few days of the event. Customers who have purchased my audio tape programmes, get sent a similar letter about 4 weeks after they have received it.

⑩ Always include a stamped self-addressed envelope. Including a business reply paid envelope could be a better option because you only pay postage on the envelopes that get used.

⑩ Remember to write a handwritten note thanking the customer for the testimonial and telling them how important they are to you. If appropriate, send a small gift. Focus on something thoughtful rather than valuable. If your gift is perceived as a 'payment', you'll undermine the gesture.

Following steps 1-3 is guaranteed to generate a steady stream of valuable testimonials you may not have received otherwise.

Step 4 - A Touch of Testimonial Sophistication

Why do people choose to do business with you?

⑩ Talk to your best customers about what went through their minds before they bought from you the first time. Interview these customers to find out what factors helped them decide to become a customer. This can be a formal market research survey, or it can be based on informal conversations over coffee. Choose the more appropriate option for your particular circumstances. Not everyone will be able to put their finger on one particular thing. It may be a combination of two or three factors. After a dozen or so conversations you should start to get a clearer idea of what goes through a prospects mind before they commit to you or your company.

⏵ Findings from a market research survey can be used to promote positive word-of-mouth amongst your target markets - but only if you score well! If the results are poorer than you hoped for, contact your customers to find ways to improve your service.

⏵ Using your research data, extract from your testimonials the comments that address the key issues your customers have identified. Construct a series of testimonials, which collectively tell prospective employers what you want them to know about you. If you were a one person business, a freelancer or 'free agent', one testimonial may focus on your high level of skill, or specialised knowledge in a particular area, another may refer to how good you are at working as part of a team, another may say that you are reliable, or how you were responsible for securing new business for them.

When you have a collection, you can either use them in their entirety, or extract the key comments you want listed on one or more sheets of paper - adverts for movies use this technique all the time - why? Because it works and it can work for you.

If you sell tangible products, customers may have stated that product quality was a key factor. Assemble a few testimonials that talk about the high quality of your products. Another factor could have been your ability to deliver to deadline on a strict budget. Compile key comments that nail that issue. If you lack testimonials covering the concerns highlighted in your research, actively seek them. When delighted customers agree to provide you with testimonials in the future, and want to know what to write for you, focus their attention on those issues on which your prospects most need reassurance.

Step 5 - USE Those Testimonials

Testimonials gathering dust in a filing cabinet are of no use to you or anyone else. Use them on just about everything seen by prospective clients. Before you use unsolicited testimonials, get permission to use them. As for those you are sent in response to a request, there's probably no need to ask for permission - it's implied within your request. But don't forget to thank the person for their support.

How and Where Can You Use Testimonials?

▶ Print them on your product packaging.

▶ Frame and display them in your office or boardroom.

▶ Incorporate them within your direct mail campaigns.

▶ Photocopy the original letters on to coloured high quality paper and mail them out to your warmest prospects.

▶ Use a text highlighter pen to mark the relevant passages.

▶ Use a rubber stamp for your testimonials that says something like "Client Testimonial". Use coloured ink to help it stand out.

▶ Extract and edit key comments to be included in your brochures, flyers and handouts.

◗ Select the most appropriate testimonials for each of your target markets. Such testimonials will reinforce your expertise within those niches.

◗ Prominently display testimonials on your website.

◗ Display a selection of testimonials in a presentation folder. Leave it on the table in your reception area for visitors to study.

◗ Carry a presentation folder with you whereever you go. Show it to all your prospects. I heard of someone who made a point of excusing himself for the bathroom whilst in the middle of a meeting, but not before he had offered his presentation folder for everyone to read while he was out of the room. He came to realise that if they were still reading the testimonials when he returned, they were ready to agree a deal. If they weren't reading it – they needed more convincing – Or he'd taken too long in the loo!

◗ Add the person's photograph to the testimonial if they have no objections. Some will be very pleased to receive the attention and recognition.

◗ Transcribe any audio and video testimonials so they can be used more widely.

◗ Some referral sources may not feel confident about their judgement. How sure are they that you and your company offer a good service? What if you don't? What if you are unprofessional or unethical? They'll look stupid to their contacts. Share your collection of testimonials with your referral sources. They will help to reassure them that their feelings about you are accurate and well founded.

Step 6 - Write Testimonials for Others

⏵ Offer to write testimonials for your favoured suppliers. It will mean as much to them as it does to you.

⏵ Please write a testimonial for this book (if you think one is deserved). Email it to Roy@RoySpeaks.com. The best ones will be uploaded to the website. They go a long way towards helping potential customers decide if this book will be of value to them too.

High Tech Testimonials

Seeking and using written testimonials is still the most common approach. However, as more and more businesses use multi-media within their marketing presentations, why not consider using audio and video testimonials? High quality audio and video recording equipment has dropped in price, and is well within the reach of most businesses. The software to edit your material is surprisingly quick and easy to use.

In the last year I started asking my regular clients if they would be prepared to record a testimonial for me. My first 'guinea pig' was the Group Chief Executive of a major British pension provider. He instantly agreed. I had explained that I would edit out the questions and asked him to incorporate the gist of my question at the beginning of his answers. Using my mini-disc recorder, (thank you Sony – I really love that machine!) and speaking in the third person, I asked him a number of questions about what 'Roy Sheppard' helped him achieve within his company. His answers talked about me in the third person too. I could not have wished for any better comments. Thank you Keith Satchell of Friends Provident.

His comments were edited down and began a collection of other audio testimonials which were subsequently uploaded to my website. Video testimonials have followed. They are all very powerful. Could you do the same?

What about:-

⏩ If you make presentations using a laptop computer, think how you could liven them up using audio and video clips from delighted customers. You are limited only by your imagination.

⏩ If you can collect a number of audio or video testimonials, you might consider producing a short programme for prospects. At the end of the programme offer a really good deal - perhaps a free gift. Don't advertise or promote the offer anywhere. When someone claims the offer, you will know they listened to or watched the programme to the end. They are more likely to be converted into a customer. Ask other customers if they would like to be included in future editions of the programme.

More Thoughts on Testimonials

⏩ If you work primarily in a B2B (Business to Business) environment rather than B2C (Business to Consumer), your testimonials carry more weight and credibility when supplied by senior individuals within other organisations.

⏩ A testimonial without the writer's name attached is not worth using. ALWAYS include the person's name and, whenever possible, their title as well as the company name.

⏩ If your business is primarily B2C, seek out influential, powerful and high profile people. Include them within your local or regional community, as well as celebrities. Celebrities who are paid to speak well of your products are providing a 'paid for endorsement', NOT a testimonial. If a celebrity gives permission for you to use a positive quote without a HUGE fee attached, when you use the comment tell your readers that it isn't a 'paid for endorsement', adding that the celebrity is so impressed with the product they offered to provide their endorsement for free. This will add a great deal to its power.

- Don't talk yourself out of asking for testimonials. A lack of self-confidence or your 'belief' that people would be unwilling to supply them, could be your biggest hurdle. Therapists in particular find it difficult to ask clients for testimonials, because of the nature of the work they do. Who wants the world to know that they've been to see a therapist? Let your customers decide. Or are you too afraid of rejection?

- Should your testimonials be dated? Interesting question. If you use the original letter, the date of the letter will be seen. When you extract key comments from a variety of sources, the date does not have to be included. Does it matter? Yes. If you were to read a testimonial that was seen to be say, 10 years old, what would you think? Probably you'd say "*That's a long time ago - I wonder why this company isn't using more recent comments? Don't they have any? Do they live in the past? Why aren't recent customers prepared to do this? It's obvious this company isn't any good!*" Dated testimonials can create confusion and uncertainty. If you can, omit the date. If you provide technology products and an old testimonial describes your company as 'leading edge' and it was written more than a year ago, it would be dishonest to keep using it. Time sensitive testimonials need to be up-to-date.

I have a lot of high quality testimonials from past clients. Some of these testimonials were written many years ago. They describe my work as a business speaker and conference moderator in glowing terms. Am I going to stop using them just because they were offered a while ago? No way! If they thought I was good then, I know I'm better now. I have even more experience and skill - not less. For you to get a sense of how powerful testimonials can be visit www.RoySpeaks.com/testimoni.htm There are 16 pages of them.

Finally, we all have 'bad' days when things don't go the way we might choose. Get out your testimonial file and read about how wonderful your customers think you are. You'll feel much better.

Chapter 6

Your PeoplePortfolio® Referral Plan

Part 4 - Behind Your Back

As part of your Behind Your Back Campaign, you and your business will benefit from being featured within articles and on programmes in the media. The more people who hear about you in a positive way, the higher your chances of being referred.

Your aim should be to get your name or your business featured in the maximum number of publications, read by your existing and prospective customers. If you are planning to enter new markets, this exercise is particularly valuable.

Competitors face a psychological disadvantage when they see your name in print on a regular basis. This chapter tells you how to go about promoting your business within your chosen niches. It's easier than you may think – but only when you know the media 'rules'. Even though results may take some time, it's almost certainly worth investing some time and effort developing relationships with selected journalists.

First of all find out:

▶ The names of the industry or trade publications your customers and prospects read, and the titles of those they subscribe to (these are usually the more important ones). Ask your customers what they read.

▶ Ask why they read them.

⏺ Define the strengths and weaknesses of each publication.

⏺ What business related websites do they regularly visit?

⏺ Call the advertising department of the publications whose names feature most prominently in your research. Ask for the following information; circulation (ignore any 'readership' number – this is a guess and doesn't tell you anything), mailed circulation (some trade publications are sent out for free, paid for from advertising revenue), who is the publication aimed at, and at what level within an organisation (you want to know how many decision makers receive and read it). Ask to be sent a Media Pack. This will include published advertising rates, and a sample copy of the publication.

Based on this research;
⏺ Clearly define the publications you want to be featured in during the next 12 months.

⏺ You may end up with a long list. This can be intimidating. PR expert Sue Spenceley Burch recommends creating an ABC prioritised list;

⏺ Your A list will be the most important publications. Press releases to these always receive telephone follow up. Relationships with journalists from these publications are developed proactively.

⏺ Those on your B list are followed up if possible,

⏺ while those on C are mailed, but not followed up.

⏺ Scan the editorial pages and note the names of the most prolific journalists. Whose work do you respect the most?

- Decide to get to know these people. A great way to meet them is at industry conferences. Help these journalists by asking who they want to meet and what information they are looking for. Don't 'sell' yourself. You'll stand out in their minds, because nearly everybody else does!

- Important; Who do you know already who also knows these people, and would be prepared to make an introduction?

- Decide how you could be seen to be a valuable resource to the readers of each publication. Study the types of articles featured.

- Brainstorm topics you have detailed knowledge about that are relevant to the reader. What could you do that is different and worthy of being reported on?

Getting Into Print

There have never been so many publications to choose from. Every industry can usually boast at least two publications, sometimes many more. All of them need to fill their editorial pages with interesting articles. This represents an opportunity for you.

> *IMPORTANT; If you are a company employee, make sure you have permission from your boss to talk to the media. Some companies have strict media relations' policies.*

Editors, journalists and radio and TV programmes producers want leading edge thinking, on issues of interest and concern to the publication's readers, listeners and viewers. They want relevant stories and copy that is lucid, concise, thought-provoking, helpful, entertaining or downright funny. Stories, anecdotes, research results from surveys and case studies have a higher chance of being published than vague, self-promoting 'puff' pieces. Having been on the receiving end of thousands of press releases, you have NO idea how much rubbish gets sent out by PR companies who should know better.

However, good PR people can be invaluable. Cultivating relationships with journalists is essential, if you want to appear in print. It takes time. Competent PR professionals have already done this. They know who to call, when to call them, what they are most interested in writing about, and know exactly how to pitch stories so editors want to cover them. Find your PR professional by referral. Ask your business associates or better still, ask journalists to recommend someone they rate highly.

BY or ABOUT You?

Until you become better known in your chosen niche, most of your media profile will be based on what you submit to publications written by yourself – or have paid a freelance journalist to write. Some journalists are prepared to interview busy executives, write the article, hand it back for you to stamp your own personality on it with small changes, before sending it to an editor in your name. The journalist is paid a fee by you. This is probably not practical until you start to receive firm commissions to supply copy. To pay a journalist, only to have a speculative piece rejected, can be an expensive way to remain obscure.

Commissioned pieces are also 'spiked' or delayed, for a variety of reasons outside the editor's control. The quality of an article is not usually the reason. The first piece I ever wrote for the business section of *The Times* didn't appear on the day it was supposed to. I was devastated, wrongly assuming it was because the editor didn't like the piece. He called me later that day to say that a large advertisement had been sold which squeezed it out. My article was not time sensitive, so it was delayed for a week. If your articles fail to appear – don't take it personally.

Letters to Editors

If you've never been published, start small. Write short, pithy letters for publication to the editors of your chosen newspapers, magazines, e-zines and websites. Study the letters pages of your targeted publication. How long are they? What topics do they cover? If you know what you are talking about, have something new or controversial to say, you stand a very good chance of getting into print. Editors of trade and in-house publications face a constant struggle to fill their editorial pages with high quality material. Help them.

If you can write well, so much the better. If you can't, don't worry too much, the letter will be 'subbed' – edited for length and clarity.

But What Do You Write?

These tips apply equally for letters for publication and articles you may be commissioned to write.

▮ Read the publication thoroughly.

▮ Ask yourself what facts, viewpoints or regulatory issues have been omitted from features

▮ Do you have any specific examples that disprove what has been published? Sometimes journalists get things badly wrong. In a fair, measured way, clarify an article's shortcomings without making personal attacks on the journalist (ultimately you want to build relationships with them, not provide them with reasons to carry a grudge about you.)

▮ Rather than 'knock' what has been written, try to add

something extra. New unpublished thoughts, insight, data, and information is always appreciated and helps position you as an authoritative 'giver', not just another 'whinger'.

⏵ Wit not sarcasm is always your best weapon.

⏵ Be curious. Ask yourself what would make an interesting story. Identify the unusual in your industry. What trends have you noticed?

⏵ You want to offer enough 'meat' in what you write to be of value to the reader, but not the entire solution, so they have to contact you for more information. As a guide, offer 60% problem and 40% solution.

⏵ Always include your phone and email address. Occasionally one will be included.

Submitting Your Letter

When you submit your letter, include the phrase 'For Publication' at the top. Attach a second brief letter headed 'Not for Publication'. In one brief sentence, compliment the publication and what you like about its content or format. Add the following *"Attached is a letter you may like to consider for publication. If you are ever looking to find sources for specific stories, I have worked in this industry for 'x' years, please feel free to give me a call. I'm particularly knowledgeable on 'y' topics, so if I can ever help you with an article along those lines, I would be delighted to do so."* Position this second letter as a personal offer of help to the editor, and NOT about how wonderful you are. Whether the letter is published or not, your second letter will start to position you as an authority on your subject/industry (Important; – make sure you ARE an authority). This paves the way for the next stage in building your relationship with editors and journalists.

Follow Up

If your letter is not published, send in another letter a couple of weeks later. Persistence usually pays off.

If your letter is published, send a handwritten note immediately saying how pleased you were that it was worthy of publication. Re-state your previous offer to help them in any way.

Tell them you have a couple of ideas for articles, and that you will call to discuss them further. Do not say what the ideas are in this note. You want to have a conversation about them on the phone. If its true, add something like *"I was talking to some colleagues recently, who felt concerned about a development they have noticed within the industry which hasn't yet been covered in the press."* No self-respecting editor could ignore such a comment.

Before you send your note. Study their publication further, and brainstorm ideas for these articles.

⏺ Ask colleagues and customers what issues they think are important.

⏺ Where are the problems?

⏺ Where is the fear and anxiety within your industry?

⏺ What and where are the potential threats and unseen opportunities?

⏺ Why would readers be interested to read about them?

Working with Journalists

⏺ Generally speaking journalists are now over-worked and under-paid – in some cases, chronically. An increasing number of journalists are freelance. They are only paid for what they can sell to editors. Competition is intense. Unless you are a nationally known newspaper columnist, there are much easier ways to earn a living than as a journalist.

Journalists are paid to be cynical. The state of their industry has forced some to become bitter as well. This is sometimes reflected in their attitudes towards business and successful people.

▶ However, there are far more who work hard, and seek to write with impartiality and a genuine interest in their subjects and the needs of their readers. So, find these journalists. Befriend the best freelance journalists. Help them to make money.

▶ Find out what topics they are most interested in.

▶ Be on the lookout for stories they may be interested in writing about.

▶ With permission, put them in touch with your contacts, so they can be written about or quoted.

▶ Most publications have a 'forward planning desk', to log forthcoming events and features. Make yourself known to these people and bring things to their attention.

▶ Become a trusted resource to the journalists you know and like.

▶ Generally, its not good to call a journalist late in the day – they are more likely to be working to a deadline, and will not want to talk to anyone. You run a higher risk of being turned down.

▶ When you get them on the 'phone, ask if they are free to talk. Briefly explain that you are not a PR person and have a few editorial ideas they may be interested in, which have nothing to do with yourself or your company. It's very important they know you are not simply promoting yourself. Go on to explain that a few clients have been talking about the following issues, and add that his/her readers might also be interested in articles that cover these subjects.

▮ When pitching an idea for an article, carefully think it through before you call an editor. Better still, say you need 2 minutes – and time yourself. At the end of the 2 minutes say *"My time is up. Do you need any other info?"* If interested, you will be asked a few questions to determine your depth of knowledge and whether it's worthy of space in the publication. You might be asked *"Why does the reader need to know about it? What's the new angle to the story? Who would you interview?"*

▮ Make absolutely sure they haven't already covered it! Nothing will destroy your credibility quicker if you didn't know.

▮ By offering two or three ideas you increase the chances of one being taken up.

▮ Don't be too disappointed if the ideas are turned down. Gently ask why they are not suitable. You may learn something that will help you offer more appropriate ones in the future.

▮ If you get a positive response, you have a few choices; offer to write it or volunteer yourself as a source. As the writer you have control, as a potential interviewee you don't. You want to write the piece, but without being too pushy about it. You could say *"If you think it would help, I could write it for you. I know the people who are most knowledgeable about the subject and would like to do it."* Notice, you are positioning yourself as someone who is helping the editor.

▮ The editor may ask you to do it, or assign the story to a staff or freelance journalist, and would probably give them your name as a source to call. Make it easier for this journalist to write an interesting article. Think about useful anecdotes, examples and short snappy quotes. If appropriate, be controversial.

▶ Words of warning - assume there is no such thing as *"Off the record"* Journalists are highly skilled at putting people at their ease, so they speak more freely. Some can be so charming, but will write pure vitriol. I've been a journalist for years, but I've been stitched up by unprofessional hacks. It happens occasionally. That's the price you pay. Don't say anything you would not be happy to see attributed to you in print.

▶ If you are to write the piece - ask how many words it needs to be. And the most important question of all, *"When will you need it by -what date and by what time?"* NEVER EVER miss an agreed deadline. It is essential that you do not let the editor down. Their schedule relies on copy being delivered as promised. If you won't be able to deliver for the appointed date, don't agree to do it, or negotiate an alternative.

▶ If you agree to write the piece, ask *"Is there a fee?"* You may not care about being paid – don't share that information. The editor may offer a fee, possibly not. When negotiating, always ask for something of high value to you, but low cost to the other party. If there is no fee, politely say that you are prepared to write it on condition your name appears at the beginning of the article, and your email or phone number is included at the end.

▶ If it fits the house style of the publication, even ask if a small photo of yourself would be needed. Sometimes this will happen. It's an excellent way to raise your profile further. Make sure you have some high quality shots available. Holiday snaps will NOT do. Tip; always supply photos to the media that show you doing something – head and shoulders shots are boring. Photo editors want photographs that add interest to page layouts. They are more likely to be enlarged.

▶ Writing an article can involve quite a lot of time. You need as many tangible benefits as possible, so negotiate for them at the outset. Be polite and low key about it. You may be surprised at how much gets agreed.

▶ Confirm what you have agreed in writing. Some editors will also send you a confirmation document, formally commissioning the article and laying out the brief for the article – title, length in words, deadline etc.

▶ Suggest the names of a few people you could speak to and why you think they may be suitable. The editor may also have certain preferences. They are likely to be influential people and provide the perfect way for you to get to know them.

▶ Select key contacts and identify key influencers you don't yet know, who you would like to feature in the article. Obviously, select contacts you know and trust first. But make sure they are being included for their suitability, not just their friendship or your business relationship.

▶ Call or write to introduce yourself to your short list of interviewees. Say *"I'm so-and-so from such-and-such company. We make or offer 'x' services to our clients. I've been asked to write an article on (topic) for (name of publication) and, as you are a leading figure within the industry, I immediately thought of you as someone to interview."* This achieves a number of things; you are instantly positioned as someone potentially valuable to them, and it gives you a fantastic reason to meet up.

▶ Take notes during the interview, or better still record the conversation on to a cassette. Tell the interviewee beforehand and reassure them that you are doing it for your own personal use. It ensures you can quote them accurately whilst allowing you to concentrate on what they tell you without having to take too many notes. Learn how to use the machine before your meeting.

Ⅱ▶ Ask "Who, what, where, when, why and how" questions. Look for nuggets of insight. If you are not sure about what they mean, ask for clarification to ensure they are not mis-quoted.

Ⅱ▶ Afterwards, write a brief hand-written note, thanking them for their help. Avoid telling them when the article will appear. (It's not up to you, but the editor). Also write to thank your editor and comment favourably on what they did to improve the piece.

Ⅱ▶ If there's time before your deadline, you might offer to let interviewees see what you write before it's submitted for them to add any comments or corrections.

Ⅱ▶ Make a point of writing another hand-written 'thank you' note to interviewees when it appears. Enclose a copy of the article to each person.

Ⅱ▶ For some, you may want to meet up again to deepen the relationship. And take your referral programme forward in other ways. If you've helped them, they will be more motivated to offer help to you.

Ⅱ▶ If you can provide the type of copy sought by an editor, don't be at all surprised when you start receiving calls from them asking for your comments on related issues. By becoming a valuable resource to editors and journalists, you will increase the number of articles you are quoted in. When this happens, readers are more inclined to assume that you are a pre-eminent individual within your industry sector. You'll then get more referrals.

About You

As your reputation and profile increases, editors and journalists may choose to run pieces about you, and what you or your company does. Often, such pieces are illustrated with photos, which further enhance your profile. Profile pieces are your ultimate goal. To be written about will tell potential customers that you are a leader in your field. Consequently, you are more likely to receive referrals from these types of features.

Don't leave it to chance. Your circle of friends, colleagues and customers can play a key role as voluntary publicists, in helping you be chosen for such articles. The positive things they say about you to members of the media will eventually result in interview requests.

Having interviewed countless business owners and show business celebrities, there is one marked difference between the two. Business people don't usually prepare for interviews. (If they do, you wouldn't know it!) They talk, you listen and then work out for yourself what you want to write about. Yes, that's a journalist's job, however… celebrities, make it easier for journalists. Some would say too easy, but the point is, they know what it takes to get written about. It's show *business*, so learn from their approach. If you are asked for such an interview, ask the journalist what they want from it. Who else are they planning to talk to? Are there any particular areas they are more interested in? What can you do to help them write a better piece? Then invest some time thinking about the possible questions and your answers. Preparation will help you sound more lucid, better informed and therefore more intelligent!

Think About the Key Moments in Your Career

▮▸ What were the turning points?

▮▸ Who are the people who have influenced you the most? And why?

⏵ What were the high spots?

⏵ The low points?

⏵ What did you learn from these times in your life?

⏵ What serious and amusing stories or anecdotes can illustrate why you think and behave in the ways you do?

⏵ What trends have you noticed in your industry? What are the threats and opportunities?

You should have answers for these questions and many more like them. Prepare.

The importance of preparation cannot be over-emphasised. Pay careful attention to the impact of everything you say. Beware of offering throw away comments that can totally change the angle of the story when it's written.

Raising your profile is good for business. Whoever said *"There's no such thing as 'bad' publicity"* was wrong. Gerald Ratner managed to destroy his chain of jewellery stores, by making an ill-advised comment about selling 'crap' to his customers. An off-the-cuff remark, once published becomes permanent. It gets stored in a newspaper's archives. These 'cuttings' get used and referred to by journalists each time they decide to write about you. Ratner's previous comment in the 1980's about a prawn sandwich lasting longer than the earrings he sold, has been repeated time and again. And yet again in this book. *So, be careful.*

Making More of Your Work

Each time you appear in print, get permission from the publisher to send copies out to your customers and key prospects, with a handwritten note that simply says *"I thought you might be interested to read this article which has just appeared in [name of publication]"*. Perhaps you have thousands of customers or prospects. Might it be appropriate to send copies to them all? Possibly. Arrange with the publisher to re-print the article. You may be surprised to discover how little this can cost.

Chapter 7

Stand and Deliver – to Spread the Word

There are tens of thousands of business and social groups that meet every week. Many need speakers to inform, entertain and educate their members. Some speakers get paid, most don't. The quality of speaker is an event organiser's biggest headache. Sharing your knowledge, expertise and insight with large groups of people, who self-select themselves as being interested in your topic or business, is a fantastic way to increase your sales. If you can offer valuable information and deliver it in an engaging and entertaining way, you will open doors to unlimited business opportunities.

- DO NOT use the talk to promote yourself or your services. You will undermine rather than enhance your credibility. Instead, let the organiser tell the audience that you are an expert on your topic, and briefly tell them a little about your company and the services you offer. Provide a short, written introduction to the meeting chairperson that must be used to introduce you. Important; specify that the person who introduces you must NOT say that you have given it to them to read out! It's to help them do a great job, introducing you.

- Prepare your talk thoroughly. The best ones appear spontaneous, but obscure hours of research. When I first began earning a living as a speaker I was told *"Invest at least one hour of research for each minute you will be speaking."* I remember thinking, that's too much. Looking back, I can tell you - it's a serious under-estimation.

▮ Create a file of ideas and possible material for future talks. Ask your friends and colleagues for up to date facts and figures, anecdotes, funny one-liners.

▮ Before any event, ask the organiser for the names of a few people who are going to be there. Call them to say that you will be speaking to the group on your topic, and ask them what they are most interested in hearing about. How much do they know? At what level? How representative are they of the rest of the group? What are they confused about? Afraid of? Ask "What would you need to learn to make being at the meeting a particularly valuable use of your time?" Don't provide the answers on the phone to these people. Before you finishyour conversation, ask the person to make a point of introducing themselves to you BEFORE you speak. This way, you will know who your friends are and can refer to them during your talk. This will help you appear 'one of them'.

▮ You should be able to pack a huge amount of specially tailored, practical and invaluable information into your talk. However, you are advised to structure the content to focus slightly more on the 'problems' rather than the 'solutions'. A 60:40% balance is good. Your aim is to motivate audience members to want to start a dialogue with you, either immediately following the event or in the days or weeks after it. Telling them everything they need to know is not the best way to do this.

▮ A useful tip; Think of a real problem facing most of your audience members then say, *"I was talking to one of my clients who told me they were having difficulty with such and such - this is what we did together to solve it."* Then provide the solution. This tells the audience what you do for clients without forcing it down their throats.

◗ Build time for lots of questions into your talk. Encourage the audience to test or challenge you *"In order to make sure you get the most value from being here."* Audience members routinely regard the Q&A element of a seminar as the most useful, although you will find that few, if anyone, wants to ask questions. Be prepared for this. Either plant some good meaty questions within the audience (TV discussion shows do it, so can you!). Or prepare a short list of written questions yourself. Say *"This often happens, so here are some questions that I've been asked in the past."* Keep going back to the audience for questions. Or ask them some questions.

◗ Produce a one or two page handout, with the key points covered in the talk. Make them available on a table, rather than handing them out. This means only the most interested people will make the effort to pick one up. Alternatively, produce a

handout which covers your talk, but leaves spaces in the text for people to fill in as you provide them with the answers. This technique increases each audience member's involvement with your material. At the bottom of your handout include, *"This information has been provided free to members of [name of organisation] by [your name]"* followed by your phone number, email address and postal address. Everyone will then have your contact details.

▮▸ Alternatively, tell the audience that your business card can be found on the table at the back of the room, for anyone who would like one.

▮▸ Offer a prize. The organisers (not you) invite the attendees to put their business card into a bowl. You will make the draw - and you get to keep the business cards.

▮▸ Hold your own seminars. Invite your existing clients and encourage them to bring along friends and colleagues, who are most likely to benefit from the information on offer. Provide fantastic content. You don't have to give a talk yourself- book a good speaker to talk on a topic that's interesting and valuable to your contacts.

▮▸ At the end of a seminar, offer attendees the opportunity to recommend friends or colleagues to attend the next event. Provide them with flyers to distribute on your behalf. Do this as a service to them, not as something being done for you.

Chapter 8

Get Yourself Connected; The Do's and Don'ts of Networking

Blame it on your parents. With our personal safety in mind they brought us up to *"Never talk to strangers!"* Good advice. But not if you are trying to grow a business or increase your sales. Millions of people learned this lesson too well. Don't get me wrong, I'm not suggesting you throw caution to the wind and engage in conversations that could compromise your safety. However, if you feel varying degrees of embarrassment, discomfort or a fear of rejection when meeting new people, this chapter will help you. If this is NOT problem for you - you'll still gain new insights and ideas for your business.

I meet A LOT of people. It's my job. I came to realise many years ago that *"Who you know determines who you become in life".* Behind every successful person is a sound and well-nurtured network. The most successful people are always the best connected. They know what support and information they need and just the right people to call. They have invested in their future by realising the importance of 'getting out more'.

How well connected you are determines your access to those with the money, the most power and influence, opening up future business opportunities for you and your company. A low profile carries a high cost.

⏩ Everyone has an address book or database, but relatively few people invest the time to build their network systematically. ANYONE can be a good networker, but even many of the brightest individuals fail to make the most of this powerful resource. Some believe they are too busy, others convince themselves that they are too important.

But *"Networking"* is such a horrible term. It too often conjures up images of insincere, manipulative, self-serving and predatory individuals, constantly hunting for someone new they can sell to or extract an undeserved favour. Meeting anyone new, ineffective networkers rapidly scan a person, prejudge their usefulness, deliver their sales mantra and conduct a 'cardboard connection', by dishing out a business card before moving on to their next target. At the end of a business gathering they smugly congratulate themselves for 'working the room' so efficiently, by handing out 20 or so business cards. The only thing they are good at is wasting their time and the people that of they 'meet'.

The most effective networkers are givers. They find ways to become a valuable person, by freely giving favours, business leads, referrals, testimonials and helpful ideas. They establish themselves as facilitators and 'matchmakers'. At the end of a networking event, they judge their success not on how many cards they have given out, but how many they have *collected* and the potential relationships they have created. Collecting people and re-connecting with them is the cornerstone of any successful networker. They find a multitude of reasons to re-connect; sending handwritten notes, newspaper clippings of possible interest and valuable news and information.

When meeting someone new, distinguished networkers ask themselves *"How useful is this person to my entire network?"*. A poor networker asks *"What can this person do for me?"* The interesting point is: good networkers not only build an admirable reputation, they benefit more than those who take the more self-centred approach. For some this may require a leap of faith - but every good networker will confirm the old maxim 'what goes around comes around' is absolutely true.

At a conference where my talk was aimed at facilitating better internal networking for a large global consultancy, the partners accepted how essential their business systems were to the success of the company. When asked *"How do you gain most of your clients?"* the answer was *"Through the people we build relationships with."* *"If that's the case, why is it there is no company system for this?"* I asked. Silence.

Before a networking system can be implemented fully it's worth taking a moment to assess what stops most people from attending more networking events. Failing to see the value of a network is the first mistake.

Effective networking requires a pro-active approach to meeting new people. It's too easy to spend time talking only with colleagues you already know. I see it all too often at conferences, where a senior management team will huddle amongst themselves, seemingly incapable of stepping out of their comfort zones to connect with new colleagues, customers or suppliers.

When you meet someone new, always introduce yourself by giving your name first, to put the other person at their ease. One of the fundamental mistakes people make when they meet others is to think that should try and impress them by showing how interesting, intelligent, experienced, or desirable they are. To build rapport and lasting relationships it is far more effective for you to be interested in others. Too many people use the time when others are talking to work out what to say next.

In the past, Francis Bacon was correct to assert that *"knowledge is power"*. Today this belief stops some people from sharing it. They believe that if they keep information to themselves they will maintain power; the opposite is true. People who keep information to themselves get bypassed. They are left out of the loop.

Always be on the look out to make connections; putting people together who have complementary skills, knowledge or interests. By doing such favours without expecting a pay back, you will build up deposits in your networking 'bank account'.

⏐▶ Get out more! Attend more industry functions and general business events. You can't grow your network if you don't meet new people.

⏐▶ Write down your relationship goals. What do you want to achieve? What are your objectives, goals and priorities. Focus your thinking on WHY you want to build a bigger and better network of contacts. More business? What type of business? More of the same, or better business?

⏐▶ Carry with you: Business cards, a note pad, pen and a breath freshener.

⏐▶ Try to match the skills and knowledge of those you meet, and put them in touch with others you have already established a relationship with.

⏐▶ List the people who you believe could help you achieve your goals. Who are the most influential in your chosen field? How could you meet and get to know those individuals?

⏐▶ Identify the gaps in your network. Do you know too many people who have similar backgrounds or think the same way?. Perhaps you only know people inside your particular industry. The business world is becoming more diverse - your network should reflect this.

⏐▶ Find out who your closest friends and colleagues know. Perhaps it would be worth you getting to know more of them.

⏐▶ Think about the following questions;

   • Why should anyone want to remember you?
   • What's in it for them?

- How can you earn a place in their lives?
- How trustworthy are you?
- Do you make a point of talking well about others?
- Are people justified in thinking of you as a particular expert?
- How well does your reputation precede you?

▶ How to hold a meaningful conversation with a stranger causes untold pain and discomfort for a huge number of people. A suggestion from both *Million Dollar Prospecting Techniques* and Bob Burg's book *Endless Referrals* a suggestion to memorise and use these 10 questions in conversation.

1) How did you get started in your business?

2) What do you enjoy most about your chosen profession?

3) What separates you and your company from your competition?

4) What advice would you give someone just starting in your line of business?

5) What one thing would you do with your business if you knew it could not fail?

6) What significant changes have you seen take place in your profession or business through the years?

7) What do you see as the upcoming trends in your business?

8) How would you describe the strangest or funniest incident you've experienced in your business?

9) What ways have you found to be the most effective for promoting your business?

10) What one sentence would you like others to use when describing your business?

> *At the end of any conversation, do you tend to know more about them or do they know more about you?*

➠ Do people who know you perceive you as one of life's generous 'givers', or as someone who tends to be a selfish 'taker'. If you're perceived as a taker, people will eventually leave you out of the loop. This is a disaster for any networker.

Ask Yourself:

➠ How can you be known as someone who under-promises and over delivers?

➠ Do you show up? When you accept an invitation to a party or an event, do the hosts subconsciously doubt if you'll be there? Woody Allen once said *"80% of success is simply showing up."* Unreliable people tend to get dropped from guest lists over time. Train others to rely on your word.

➠ Who initiates most of your social or business conversations and meetings? Who invites who? If others don't extend many invitations to you, what could this be saying about you and your behaviour?

> *"The word is 'Network', not Net-sit, Net-eat or Net-drink"*
> Ivan Misner PhD

➠ My friend Ian Johnston has many wonderful qualities but one deserves a special mention. His ability to choose the perfect gift is quite remarkable. His secret? He listens very attentively to people and notices if his friends or colleagues express a particular interest in something which could be turned into a gift. He makes a mental note. Many months later on your next birthday he will hand you the perfect present.

❿ Be consistent and congruent - in other words, behave in a way that reinforces who you are or who you aspire to be.

❿ How many people do you know who would be prepared to stake their reputation on you? How many people do you know who would be prepared to stake their reputation on you?

❿ Actively promote the achievements of others.

❿ Give people enough reasons for them to speak well of you to those you have yet to meet. This word-of-mouth character endorsement is far more powerful than anything you could ever say about yourself.

❿ Attend more conferences and make a point to contribute ideas and ask questions.

❿ 'Gatekeepers' are those individuals who control access to other important people and organisations they are particularly valuable people to know and as a networker it should be your aim to become one yourself. They have enormous power and can help you gain access almost anywhere-or refuse you! If you are seen to have support from these people, you will save yourself an enormous amount of time and trouble in achieving your objectives. Doors will open miraculously for you. With this privilege comes responsibility. If you betray such trust, believing that your short term goals are more important than your long-term trustworthiness, you will do yourself more harm than good. Look after gatekeepers better than anyone else you know.

❿ Regardless of how senior you may be, who are the secretaries and assistants of those you want to forge a relationship with? They are important 'gatekeepers' and can be huge allies or formidable opponents. Don't make the mistake of taking them for granted.

▮▶ Spouses also have FAR more power and influence than some imagine. Nurture them. Get to know them as people. Look after their interests, and they will recognise and reward you by providing access to their decision making partners.

▮▶ Make a point of getting to know people from security and the post room. These individuals always know what's going on. Find out about their interests, their families. Invest time in them.

▮▶ Make it a priority to get to know all sorts of people within your own company and those you do business with.

▮▶ Your network can provide you with a life-raft to another career. During difficult times within an economic cycle, your network has the power to be your saviour. Develop it before you need it. Build it into your career plan.

▮▶ What do you need to know in order to do the best job?

▮▶ What do your colleagues need to know in order to do a better job?

▮▶ Who do you know who can offer you information and advice? All too often, we already know people with the expertise, but don't realise it. This is why it is crucial to get to know everyone in your existing network on a deeper level. You will discover hidden skills, experience and knowledge.

▮▶ Who are the individuals whose opinions are most valued in your industry? What do you need to do for those individuals so they will want to know you?

▮▶ Perhaps you work in a highly regulated environment. Which individuals and organisations have the power? Who do you know who has access to these individuals?

▮ Where would you find people with the experience you lack, and who can offer an introduction to the types of people you wish to meet?

▮ Find out what is happening in your business and make it known that you were looking for leading edge thinking on your topics. Where is your industry sector heading? What are the problems others anticipate around the corner?

▮ Encourage and reward others to feed you with valuable and up-to-date information. If your work involves making lots of decisions, the quality of information you receive has a fundamental effect on your ability to do a good job. Become a hub of information, where it flows in and out of your life. The only way you will achieve this is by being known as someone prepared to share information.

▮ Ask yourself *"Who would find this information of particular value?"* So long as it isn't confidential - share it. Proactively trade information and knowledge. Be valuable to others.

▮ Who can supply you with high quality bad news? If you are a senior person this news is often the first to be sanitised or omitted from reports and meetings. Encourage bad news from everyone, so you hear it before it has time to do any real damage. And this is an important point, ALWAYS be profuse with your thanks when you hear bad news. Never respond negatively to the person who delivers it. This valuable source will simply clam up in the future.

▮ If your company has salespeople, seek information from their customers on what the competition is doing. Anyone who has direct contact with customers is someone who can provide invaluable information. This can be a sensitive issue so don't compromise their integrity.

ⅠⅠ If in a position to hire people, find out about how well connected the candidates are. How valuable could their contacts be to your company?

ⅠⅠ When you appoint a new supplier, find out who else they know. Their contacts could be worth more to you than the actual provision of their products or services. Build this into the equation.

ⅠⅠ Who are the really good networkers inside your company, speak to them first. Find out what they do.

ⅠⅠ If it's appropriate, ask them who they think holds the perceived power and who holds the REAL power.

ⅠⅠ When you have identified people from other parts of your organisation, suggest it might be mutually worthwhile to have coffee or lunch together. When you meet, focus on what you can do to help them. Do not ask for help. You have to earn a place in their lives first. Some may be a little suspicious of your intentions. Explain that you are trying to build bridges across the organisation to find ways to work more closely together.

ⅠⅠ Identify your contemporaries and your peers. Include more people than you think you should, not just those in your department, but those in other project groups, divisions and at other locations. Add your suppliers, customers and even your competitors. Include people at your level in departments that you would never normally have anything to do with. If you work in marketing, get in touch with people in manufacturing. If those relationships don't exist - create them.

ⅠⅠ Help your peers achieve what they want. You will also increase the likelihood that you can call on them for support when you need it. You have no power over them, but you can have a massive impact on each others' work. All of these and others can become a team of people working on your behalf - but only if you are prepared to do the same for them.

▶ Regardless of your official place within an organisation, you will discover from meeting these diverse people where the problems are. Take the initiative to put together a team of volunteers to try to resolve these problems. Most senior people will applaud your initiative. This type of behaviour can look rather impressive on a formal appraisal because it demonstrates initiative, team working and looking after the interests of the company.

▶ When you talk about customers, most people think of external ones. However any individuals who need your services are customers, even though cash may not change hands. We all have internal customers and suppliers. Identify them and build more bridges

▶ Find out who the young go-getters are within your company. Those on their way up - if they aren't looked after they'll fly out of the door. They can be a valuable source of new ideas and insights, and can usually be identified as the individuals who your cynical colleagues will describe as either being too full of themselves, or have far too much enthusiasm and too many ideas. Associate with them, not the cynics. Be a valuable resource to the go-getters. One day they may end up running everything.

▶ For a month, keep a log of everyone you interact with. Then analyse these people and, if possible, categorise them - who are the givers and who are the takers? Who are valuable and who are time wasters?

▶ Identify those you support within your company and those you don't. Ask yourself why you feel this way about them.

➧ Develop a personal plan to meet with at least one person a week whom you haven't spoken to in a while, for lunch or drinks after work.

➧ Make a point of connecting with senior people and older individuals. Ask yourself what value you can bring to that relationship.

➧ What type of information do your bosses need? How can you help them get it? Don't guess, ask.

➧ Look at the strengths and weaknesses of your superiors. Ask yourself how you can complement those skills or deficiencies.

➧ What is your boss actually trying to achieve? What are their short, medium and long-term objectives? In my experience of meeting many business people, members of staff usually have no idea what their boss's agendas are. Managers can't understand why their staff won't do what is needed. It's simple - they don't know. No one has told them.

➧ Find out from your line manager, what you need to do to make them look good. Finding out the answer to this question can have a serious and positive impact on your effectiveness in the future.

➧ Another way to build closer ties between those you work with could involve creating a 'fruit forum'. What is it? A meeting of up to a dozen colleagues on a regular, casual and informal basis, where people from one or more departments can talk 'off the record' with team leaders and executives. Everyone is encouraged to share current issues, problems, referral opportunities, and work together on viable solutions. For fruit forums to work, everyone who takes part must know that what they say will never be used against them in any way - and that the senior people are committed to hearing bad news.

▶ One more point - with all the best will in the world - if you do what I've just been talking about -accept that some people won't want to know. They are not interested in anything or anybody more than 6 feet away from their work area. If this happens - it's probably nothing to do with you. Don't let it, or them, stop you.

▶ Get to know your suppliers better. You will both save money and time, whilst simultaneously improving the quality of your products and services. Build a relationship and ask them to recommend you - if you win, so do they.

▶ Get out more to trade shows and conferences, either as a delegate or as a speaker. Study the catalogues, delegate lists and brochures before you go, to formulate a plan, to make it a valuable investment of your limited time and money.

▶ Ask for a delegate list in advance if you are attending a seminar or conference. Use the list to target those you want to meet.

▶ Decide that you will stay until you have met and connected with a pre-determined number of people. Start with just one or two - as your confidence and success grows, build it up to five or six.

▶ Listen more carefully to others' names. Repeat them until they are lodged in your brain. If you didn't catch it, ask them to repeat it, rather than 'letting it go'.

▶ Focus on finding ways to be of value to others. Forget, initially what's in it for you. Do this by offering opportunities to others –

information, referrals and recommendations – with little or even no desire for 'a return favour'. Offers with strings attached are not offers.

◗ Teach your colleagues, staff and family the benefits and skills of networking. Your own networking will become far more effective when those around you know how to build relationships.

◗ Keeping in touch with your contacts People move on more than ever before. Many get promoted and therefore, have more responsibility, a higher authority - and bigger budgets - some of which can be spent with you.

◗ Don't spray your business cards around like a tom cat!

◗ Don't introduce a female colleague by only her first name, when men are so often given the works - full name, job title and why they are so successful or important.

◗ Do not contact others only when you want something - people notice.

◗ One final thought, courtesy of Ralph Waldo Emerson "If you want a friend, be one."

This chapter is based on Roy Sheppard's seminar and four part audio programme "Network to Win". Further details can be found at the end of this book.

Chapter 9

On-Line Referrals

No up-to-date book on referrals can ignore the role of the internet, in delivering additional sales. There are hundreds, even thousands of high traffic sites that could be selling your products and services for you, as part of an affiliate, referral or revenue sharing programme. But why would they? Simple. They earn a referral fee or commission for each sale they originate for you. 8-15% commissions are commonplace. Some referral programmes pay for actual sales, leads, per enquiry or per 'click-through'.

Similarly, if your site has high traffic you could be selling products and services that complement your own offering. Select non-competing products your customers might normally buy, before, alongside or after they've bought from you. Add these products and services to help your existing and future customers. If it's good for you, invite those suppliers to include your products within their portfolio. Both parties benefit. Do it with a larger number of suppliers and your sales could sky-rocket. This need not be confined to your on-line business.

It's a simple, yet revolutionary business model originated by on-line book retailer Amazon.com. They reward other web owners to send them customers. Their growing network of over 40,000 UK associates and 500,000+ in the United States, is the largest in the world and makes a significant contribution to their annual turnover. A programme of support for affiliates includes weekly newsletters, suggestions for specific products, a 'Site of the Week' award and money - for some, lots of it. At the time of writing, they pay 5% for everything except books. Books that link directly to Amazon and show discounts of 10, 20 or 30%, earn a 15% referral fee.

Elly Russell, Head of Associates Programme for Amazon.co.uk, says *"There are some great websites as part of our associate programme so the 'Site of the Week Award' not only highlights them to our other associates, but sending traffic to each other, they all learn from one another. Everyone benefits."* On how associates succeed she adds *"Take a gardening site as an example, they might feature articles on a particular aspect of gardening and, where appropriate, weave book or video recommendations within the text. Their credibility and authority on the subject carries a lot of weight with the visitor."* Obviously, if this is ever betrayed, you lose the customer forever. Affiliate programmes only work when there is a high degree of trust between website owner, visitor and the affiliate partner. It's that loyalty that extends the visitor to the other website, rather than an impersonal, unendorsed banner advertisement.

The basic concept has been taken up by a myriad of other well known businesses. Could yours? Such joint ventures can be mutually beneficial for providers, website owners and web visitors. Affiliate guru Declan Dunn recommends *"Build a sales force of affiliates that believe in what you are offering, and back them up with a system that automates the advertising, selling, and delivery of your product line. Make it easy for your affiliates, and their customers, to work with you."*

As well as the obvious financial benefit to a website owner, there are other benefits to consider. Many sites are too small to be taken seriously as a banner advertiser, traffic may fluctuate and it involves too much time and effort for the owners to convince potential advertisers to book space, and then re-book it. With an affiliate programme, it costs less for a company to participate, therefore it's an easier sell and the site can show more interesting and dynamic content. That increases its value to visitors.

But before you jump in by creating or signing up for any affiliate programmes, do some basic on-line research. Not all products and services lend themselves to being purchased in this way. You need to be confident that there is a market for your offering, customers are happy to buy it on-line, and your most likely affiliates would be interested in partnering with you. Selling something costing hundreds or thousands of pounds/dollars to someone who doesn't know you, probably won't work. The risk is too high for the website visitor. But a relatively inexpensive item, not easily available to the buyer, lowers the risk. Including testimonials, your postal address on every page and pictures of staff members, will all contribute to a sense that you are a genuine and trustworthy business.

How to do it:-

◗ Get online and behave like a customer. How would you go about finding yourself on the web? Experiment with different search words.

◗ Where do you end up?

◗ Whose names keep cropping up as 'influencers' in your field? (Other than yourself of course!) If your name does not appear, perhaps your website has not been submitted to the search engines and directories. It is a simple process. Search the web for advice on how to do it.

◗ How could you partner with influencers?

◗ Who are already selling to those customers you would most like to reach?

◗ What sites are the most trusted resources to your target customers?

◆ Which ones have the highest traffic?

◆ Focus on attracting websites that have a narrow focus and clearly target the same types of people you do. Avoid general sites that try to appeal to everyone - they don't. And people won't buy. And the site owner will blame you for a lousy affiliate programme. Stay focused.

◆ Contact the most appropriate sites with a personal, not automated, email. Explain who you are, why you visited their site, what you are suggesting and why you think it could be in both your interests to do this. Be low key about it. They don't know or trust you yet. So don't promise anything or try too hard a sell. It will put them off. If you don't get a response within a few days - send another email. Or try to telephone the person, if that's possible. Your aim; to build up trust and demonstrate that it is in their interests to become an affiliate.

◆ Eliminate all risk to them. Prove that you are professional and ethical, that there's a real demand for your products and services, from a significant proportion of visitors to their site and, with the owner's blessing, that visitors would appreciate the opportunity to buy.

◆ When a web owner signs up as an affiliate, you need to provide them with a tracking number, so you will know each time one of their visitors arrives at your site to purchase a product. Each transaction would include this number, allowing you to notify web owners automatically every time a sale is made. Their commissions are then calculated automatically.

◆ By providing additional information to web owners, such as how many people are directed to your site by each affiliate, how long they stay and how many buy something, will have a major impact on the success or failure of any affiliate programme. It helps them to know what is working and what isn't. This data is invaluable for you too. You will learn which affiliates are generating the most/least business.

◗ Offer a very limited number of products. Too much choice is confusing - for both the web owner and visitors. A web owner is more likely to say "No" if you suggest they carry your entire catalogue. Which products are low cost but could lead to additional sales? The secret is to increase trust and, therefore ,generate repeat customers. Your profit will come when you sell repeatedly to each customer.

◗ Provide your affiliates with banner ads, photographs of each product, articles related to what you offer for them to upload to the site or for inclusion in their newsletters and e-zines, as well as your sales and marketing copy. Make it easy for them. If your product is more intangible, supply photos of customers, together with their testimonials. Make these types of product as real as you can.

◗ Persuade web owners to try your product themselves. If satisfied, encourage them to write a personal endorsement for it on their site. A testimonial will go a long way towards persuading visitors to make a buying decision. An endorsement from a trusted individual can make all the difference to a sale. If they don't like your product - the affiliate programme is probably dead. Improve your product or move on.

◗ By automating the entire process you can invite all visitors to join your email list to receive newsletters or new product information. Each time you send out a follow up email with relevant, useful information, you increase that visitor's level of trust. It's what Seth Godin, the author of *Permission Marketing* describes as *"Turning strangers into friends and friends into customers."* It may take four or five follow-ups to motivate a visitor to make a purchase. The affiliate's tracking number ensures they are rewarded for directing that person to your site. Your task is to earn the visitor's trust, demonstrate value, offer a high degree of customer service and create an environment in which they choose to buy from you again - and tell all their friends about it too!

Affiliate programmes are a valuable addition to any referral programme. A decision to build a network of inter-related businesses, that passes business via affiliate programmes could make a significant contribution to 'web-friendly' businesses.

Because the topic is changing so quickly, check out www.RoySpeaks.com/refer.htm for the latest examples, resources and information on affiliate and on-line referral programmes.

Appendix

Strategic Questions

As a professional interviewer I learned years ago - Ask a vague question, you get a vague answer. Ask a focused question, you get a more focused answer. I also discovered that just about everyone has the answers to most of their problems, they simply don't ask themselves the best questions.

The questions on the following pages have been designed to help provoke you and clarify your thinking about referrals. This will help you make more strategic business decisions based on data and information rather than a 'gut feeling'. You will be better equipped to make more of referral opportunities for your unique circumstances. If you don't know the answer - don't guess. Do some research.

Select and answer the most appropriate questions for you:

- What proportion of your business is generated by referrals?
- Where does your business come from?
- How much does it cost you to acquire?
- Conservatively, what proportion could be generated by referral?
- What's a good referral?
- Who do you aspire to do business with?
- Who do you know who has experience dealing with such companies?
- Why do people buy from you and not anyone else? What do they get out of the experience?

- Which professions or sectors do specialise in, or would like to?
- Who are the most influential leaders in your industry?
- Which professions or sectors do specialise in, or would like to?
- Who DON'T you want as clients and why?
- What groups of people already exist who you can target? This will accelerate the number of referrals you attract from the individuals within those groups.
- What new products and services could you develop specifically for customers who would be motivated to refer you on to others?
- How would you clearly define your preferred customers in writing? Circulate this profile to your key contacts.
- What is the full value in terms of future fees, profit and referrals from each new client or customer?
- Which professions or organisations could you develop joint alliances by 'Cross Referring' business to each other?
- Ask yourself what would it take for you to become the best at what you and your company does. This will radically improve your chances of increased referrals.
- Who are more successful at what you do - locally, regionally and nationally?
- What do they do differently/better? Study and 'model' (copy) them.
- In which ways are your products, services and terms better?
- What do you need to do in order for your customers to say that it is such a pleasure to do business with you?
- What do you need to stop doing for this to happen more?
- Where are you most likely to receive the most or the best referrals?
- What could you do on a regular basis to actively seek opportunities for giving and receiving referrals?
- What are the key skills of those in your networks?
- How clear are others in terms of what you want. In defining your best prospects and your most valuable information?

- Which areas of your network are you short?
- Think ahead-what will you need in the next year? Funding? People? Advice? Information? Research? Business Intelligence? Analysis?
- Who do you need to know in the next 12 months?
- What new niche markets could you focus on?
- What do people say about you behind your back?
- What do you need to change within your business, to ensure that others speak well of you?
- What advice and services can you and your company foresee needing in the future?
- How many people do you know who left your industry? Where do they now work? Would they be willing to allow you to tap into their new Networks? What's in it for them?
- How do you, or could you reward those who give you referrals?
- How easy is it for people to give you referrals?
- What system do you have for capturing and following up leads and referrals?
- Why should anyone think of you and your business when they need or meet someone who needs what you offer?
- What are most effective ways you acquire referrals currently? Verbally? In writing? From network clubs and organisations? From friends and customers anyway? Online? At events and seminars? Reward or incentive schemes?
- Who would it be appropriate to offer fees for those who refer you?
- Who would it NOT be appropriate to offer fees?
- Who are the sources for the best referrals at the moment? Friends, colleagues, customers, suppliers, network members?
- Who within your network don't offer referrals? Why is this?
- How clear are others about what you want?
- What do customers do immediately before and after they have bought from you?

- Who can tell you what your competition is doing?
- What's holding you back from asking for referrals? Have a discussion amongst your colleagues.
- What do people need in order to motivate them to share their own contacts with you?

Customer questions

- Find out how each of your customers came to do business with you.
- What role did your advertising and marketing efforts have on persuading them to do business with you?
- How many based their decision on the thoughts and opinions of others?
- Who were they?
- What relationship did they have with these people?
- What did they hear about you 'behind your back' that led to their decision to do business with you/your company? And from how many people?
- What new information do you need to know about your customers?
- What does fantastic service mean to your clients?

Being of Value to your Network and Customers

- What can you do to help your existing customers, key influencers and network members to make more money?
- What business do they want more of?
- What customers DON'T they want?
- Who are the people you would be most inclined to help? Which friends? Colleagues? Customers? Suppliers?
- What turns them on outside work and business?
- How could you make each person look good to colleagues, bosses and their customers?
- What are your contacts most proud of?

Index

INDEX